MATTHEW J. PALLAMARY

Phantastic Fiction

A Shamanic Approach to Story

by

Matthew J. Pallamary

Mystic Ink Publishing

MATTHEW J. PALLAMARY

Mystic Ink Publishing
San Diego, CA
www.mysticinkpublishing.com

ISBN 10: 0692361243 (sc)
ISBN 13: 978-0692361245 (sc)
Printed in the United States of America
North Charleston, South Carolina

This book is printed on acid-free paper made from 30% post-consumer waste recycled material.

Library of Congress Control Number: 2015900803

Book Jacket and Page Design: Matthew J. Pallamary/San Diego CA
Author's Photographs: Matthew J. Pallamary -- Gibbs Photo/Malibu CA

DEDICATION

This book is dedicated to Colleen Kennedy, Eric Hart, Ken Reeth, Charles M. Schulz, Barnaby Conrad, Charles Champlin, and Ray Bradbury.

ACKNOWLEDGEMENTS

The author wishes to acknowledge the support of Rob Gubala, Kim Gubala, Margaux Hession, Colleen Pallamary, The Santa Barbara Writer's Conference, and The Southern California Writer's Conference.

MATTHEW J. PALLAMARY

Author's Note

This book defines the essence of what a story is and is written with a focus toward writing novels. Most of its concepts also apply to screenwriting, short stories, and plays. Many of the ideas shared here overlap and are repeated to emphasize their importance. For the sake of simplicity, any references to man or woman can be used interchangeably.

MATTHEW J. PALLAMARY

TABLE OF CONTENTS

FOREWORD

I have been teaching what has come to be known as the Phantastic Fiction workshop at the Santa Barbara Writer's Conference and the Southern California Writer's Conference for twenty five years as of this writing. This book comes from what I have been blessed to have learned from my many mentors, among them Ray Bradbury, Charles (Sparky) Schulz, Barnaby Conrad, Sid Stebel, Chuck Champlin, Abe Polsky, Victor Villasenor, David Brin, Stanley Krippner, and Joan Oppenheimer as well as the many students who have come to my workshops through the years.

My students have been my greatest teachers.

I also took an honors course in anthropology at San Diego Mesa College from professor Chuck Wallace called "A Forest of Symbols - Orientation and Meaning to South American Indian Religions", which inspired me to write my historical novel, **Land *Without* Evil** about the conflict between the religious beliefs of the Guarani Indians in South America and the Jesuits, told from the Indian's point of view.

I have researched shamanism extensively and in my studies I discovered that the majority of contemporary religious thought is based on the written words of prophets who have had their revelations recorded and passed down through generations, which means they have been interpreted and reinterpreted numerous times, diluting and distorting their original meaning.

Shamanism is based on direct experience.

Shamans don't learn from books, they learn from personal, subjective visionary experiences by pushing their bodies, minds, and spirits beyond the limits of rational thought in order to transcend the confines of logical, linear thought that western culture embraces at the expense of emotion and intuition.

I have "walked with my feet on both paths" and have spent extended time in the jungles, mountains, and deserts of North, Central, and South America pursuing my studies of shamanism and ancient cultures. Through my research into the written word, direct experience, and the ancient beliefs of shamanism, I have uncovered the heart of what a story *really* is and integrated it into core dramatic concepts that have their basis in shamanism.

Central to shamanic thought is the concept of transformation which is the essence of Joseph Campbell's Hero's Journey, which is also the essence of story.

Matthew J. Pallamary   February 14, 2015

INTRODUCTION

A World Made of Language

The evidence gathered from millennia of shamanic experience argues that the world is actually made of language. Although at odds with the expectations of modern science, this radical proposition is in agreement with much of current linguistic thinking.

Boston University anthropologist Misia Landau stated that, "The twentieth-century linguistic revolution is the recognition that language is not merely a device for communicating ideas about the world, but rather a tool for bringing the world into existence in the first place. Reality is not simply 'experienced' or 'reflected' in language, but instead is actually produced by language."

In **Food of the Gods**, Terence McKenna wrote, "From the point of view of the psychedelic shaman, the world appears to be more in the nature of an utterance or a tale than in any way related to the leptons and baryons or charge and spin that our high priests, the physicists, speak of. For the shaman, the cosmos is a tale that becomes true as it is told and as it tells itself. This perspective implies that human imagination can seize the tiller of being in the world. Freedom, personal responsibility, and a humbling awareness of the true size and intelligence of the world combine in this point of view to make it a fitting basis for living an authentic neo-Archaic life. A reverence for and an immersion in the powers of language and communication are the basis of the shamanic path."

The implications of a shamanic point of view take on greater meaning in light of the rapidly changing technological world that we live in. Einstein's theory of relativity changed the concept of reality as we know it. Our perception of the world underwent a radical change from Newtonian physics to relativistic physics, and our whole reality changed as the result of one man's thoughts.

What are thoughts and how are they expressed?

Language.

Words are expressed thoughts. Put them together coherently and you weave a reality that can be conveyed to others through a common medium that humanity has accepted as a primary means of communication. The reality you create can be an account of a real event, or it can be made up from the landscape of your mind.

Fiction is something made up from nothing. Its very definition implies something not based on fact, but who says it cannot contain truth? In essence, fiction is a way of seeing the world filtered through the perception and mind of the author, or better still the minds of his or her characters.

Fiction can bring order to a chaotic world.

When writers create fictional worlds, we are the God or Goddess of those worlds, in complete control of the lives and destinies of our characters. Our creations. If, as shamans believe, there is one unifying universal intelligence that connects us all to each other and the world that we inhabit, then this is the creator of all that we know, and when we choose to create, we are emulating this force. We create our own universes which we have total control over. This action allows us to *dramatize* our truth, whether "universal" or personal, and put our thoughts in the hearts and minds of others, influencing the way that they perceive reality -- changing their reality.

Make no mistake about it. This is magic. Words *spelled* out with letters create a *spell*. Sleight-of-hand magicians, illusionists, shamans, and writers weave spells by working with the malleable texture of perception. This is the core concept behind what is called "suspension of disbelief", a necessary element of a fiction writer's repertoire, especially in literature of the fantastic.

This magical act of prestidigitation acts as a bridge, bringing forth inner worlds from the minds of their creators through the medium of words, creating a separate reality, or a spell formed by the creator. This shamanic journey through infinite inner worlds and the subsequent return "home" forms the basis for Joseph Campbell's

Hero's Journey, the cornerstone of what we know of as Story.

Like the mythical hero, shamans act as bridges between these worlds. Through strict discipline they learn to free themselves from the restrictions of "ordinary reality", transcending time and space to fly to other worlds seeking spiritual knowledge, then returning to consensual reality, bringing the wisdom gained from their visionary experience back to this world to share with others -- which is the same thing writers do with their own personal visions. Through discipline shamans transcend their selves and the boundaries that bind them by following and learning the rules and then breaking them -- only after mastering them.

So it is with fiction writers.

Musicians learn chords and scale progressions, dancers refine their steps, and martial artists perfect their kicks, punches, and forms. Each kick, punch, dance step, or note is a word. Put together, they form songs, dances, katas, and sentences. Statements.

Dedicated artists practice their basics diligently, but when it is time to perform, there is no thought of basics. Instead, they go with the flow, staying in the timeless now, being alive in the moment of creation where worlds come into being seemingly from nothing.

This is the moment of process that true artists live for. Many think of this timeless magic moment as channeling a higher power, or to some a direct line to their muse. The journey to the effective use of the gift of creation is by necessity a long arduous roller coaster ride of sacrifice, bringing the highest of highs, and the lowest of lows that can blow your ego all out of proportion in one moment and crush it in humiliation the next.

It takes many things to be a successful writer. Aside from an obsessional desire, you must have a healthy ego, be street smart, and be a businessman. You have to be a warrior, an artist, a storyteller, a salesman, a critic, a craftsman -- and you have to believe in yourself and what you have to say. Above all, you have to love the language.

If you have the qualities listed above, then like it or not, you are a modern day shaman and what follows has been written for you.

The World's Oldest Profession

The World's Oldest Profession is not what we have been led to believe by that old time worn cliché. *Shamanism* is the world's oldest profession. Throughout every world culture, shamans were the first doctors, psychologists, teachers, artists, musicians, performing artists, and yes -- storytellers. The roots of these traditions goes back to pre-history.

Shamanism evolved from the first moments of self-awareness when humans looked up at the stars to question the meaning of existence. These roots and the patterns they engender are buried deep in our individual and collective psyches. Every single religion and mode of religious thought has its roots in shamanism.

There are fundamental elements to a shamanic world view that still ring true today. Many which shamans have known for millennia are now being "discovered" in the world of quantum physics. Central to shamanic thought is the concept of transformation which is the essence of the Hero's Journey, the essence of story.

The reason these elements ring true to the core of our being both collectively and individually is because they touch on what we think of as universal patterns and concepts known as archetypes.

According to Wikipedia the concept of an archetype is found in areas relating to behavior, modern psychological theory, and literary analysis.

An archetype can be:

1. a statement, pattern of behavior, or prototype which other statements, patterns of behavior, and objects copy or emulate;
2. a Platonic philosophical idea referring to pure forms which embody the fundamental characteristics of a thing;
3. a collectively-inherited unconscious idea, pattern of thought, image, etc., that is universally present in individual psyches, as in Jungian psychology;
4. or a constantly recurring symbol or motif in literature, painting, or mythology (this usage of the term draws from both comparative anthropology and Jungian archetypal theory).

Star Wars, **Harry Potter**, and **The Lord of the Rings** all became wildly popular in modern times because the journey of the protagonists in these stories followed the path of the Hero's Journey and hit upon the archetypes that resonated with their audiences on a deep subconscious level. In ancient times, **The Iliad**, and **The Odyssey**, two of western cultures most enduring myths also followed this path, as did the creation myths of advanced cultures or those of "primitive" rain forest tribes. The principles at work in these stories provide the overall plotting structure that guides the arc of the protagonist and his or her transformation.

When you analyze all of the components that are utilized in the creation of a story there are numerous elements endemic to shamanism that come into play. Once you are aware of them, you can use them to energize your story so that it "pops" off the page or screen and comes to life in the minds of your audience.

Skillful application of these concepts along with other proven storytelling techniques will allow your audience to immerse themselves in the spell of the world you have created, allowing them to suspend their disbelief and become absorbed in your creation so they can live vicariously through the adventures of your hero by experiencing the world through their perceptions.

The concept of the shaman as a bridge between the worlds is a central idea that defines shamanism. Whether journeying through the spirit world to gain knowledge about healing, or to seek out lost souls in a process called soul retrieval, like the hero on his quest, the shaman must undergo a series of ordeals in the physical, spiritual, and psychological realms to gain access to hidden knowledge that holds the key to power.

In order to become a man of power, a shaman must travel to the underworld where he faces an ordeal of dismemberment, whether it is by being swallowed by a jaguar, which is a common theme in South American shamanism, or some other all-encompassing radical transformation that destroys him like the phoenix in a fire so he can be reborn in a new, more powerful form. This path to destruction and rebirth is referred to as the power path.

In many shamanic cultures, particularly those in the rain forests of South America, the person seeking healing brings their troubles to the shaman. Instead of dispensing medicine to treat the symptoms of the malady the way doctors in the western allopathic model of healing do, *the shaman is often the one who takes the medicine to find a cure for that individual*, allowing them to become the bridge between the spiritual and material worlds.

This act of bridging worlds is what the author/creator does with their words when they successfully orient their audience, essentially immersing them in the world of their hero, allowing them to access to the thoughts, feelings, and other direct perceptions that the hero experiences.

How these words are used and how this message is delivered are the keys to what makes the reality that you create come to life in the hearts and minds of your audience. Understanding the world view of a shaman and learning to see things from their perspective brings insight to this process. No matter what you may believe, the truth is that we create the reality that we experience in our minds where all the inputs we receive are filtered and sorted to bring order to the universe that we are at the center of.

In other words, *the center of the universe is right between your eyes*, which is where it exists for the point of view characters that you create.

As writers it is our job to deliver the most effective input possible through the selection of details that we provide so that our audience can experience the reality that we wish to convey in a fictional dream or spell that allows them to suspend their disbelief and participate in the world or worlds that we want to create.

The act of reading (and watching film to some degree) is an act of co-creation between the writer and their audience. It is up to the writer to supply the *significant details* that allow the reader to bring their own unique and individual interpretation to the experience, guided by the cues the writer provides. This is why you often hear conflicting opinions about films and books. What one person hates, another person loves. These interpretations are based on individual tastes and subjectivity. Someone who has been the unfortunate victim of a rape will have a completely different reaction to a rape scene than someone who has never experienced it.

Another way of looking at this is to see the mind as a canvas or screen where the words, phrases, and sentences are the strokes of a brush that provide the details that bring a complete subjective experience on a visual, emotional, all-encompassing, experience that moves the audience in a dynamic way.

The key to this is movement of words, phrases, and sentences is an indicator of energy, which is what they represent, and subsequently what brings a story to life. Your creation must be dynamic and moving as opposed to static and unmoving. You don't want your audience to be sitting in awe of your beautifully crafted words the way patrons of a museum admire a beautifully crafted painting on a canvas. You want them caught up and engaged in an active, shifting progression that takes them on a journey and provides them with a literal moving experience.

Process

What motivates a person to write?
Many people get caught up in the fantasy of "getting published" or they traipse from writer's conference to writer's conference, "being a writer", their main goal to win a coveted fiction award. There are some who never write all year, go to a conference and spend the whole week or weekend in a semi-sleepless frenzy, writing first chapters, openings, and short stories. You see them reading the same short stories year after year, taking their strokes. After reading the same story repeatedly in writing work shops, they have a highly polished gem that they continue to read so they can get an award and more attention.

There are people who write simply for the joy of it without an eye toward serious publication such as journal writers, poets, and short story writers. Because they do not spend as much time at their craft as novelists, they do not get as deep into the craft as novelists, who by the very immensity of their undertaking, devote considerable time and energy to their writing.

If a person thinks they have talent for writing, they should pursue it, but if they want to be a novelist, they had better bring the full force of their energies to it, because it is not for the faint of heart. Aside from the shark-infested, treacherous waters of trying to get published and noticed, producing new material is hard work. Committed writers recognize kindred spirits at conferences and gravitate toward them. It's a shame for the dilettantes, because the pseudo-writers miss out on the real joy of writing.

The process.

The creative moment where their visionary experience comes into being in this world.

The no-man's land, the nether world, that terrifying void between the opening of your story and the ending. *This is the place where the magic happens.* You've managed a start and you have an idea of where you want to go, but you have no idea how you're going to get there, so you stare at the blank page or screen, waiting for your subconscious to regurgitate something meaty. If you're a committed writer you've learned to feed, train, and trust your mind, and when it delivers you understand that what springs forth is part of the emptying out process, putting forth bits and pieces of all the things you fed your subconscious in the initial research part of the process.

The major difference between a professional and a dilettante is that the amateur waits around for the wings of inspiration to raise them up to that magical place of creation, while the professional disciplines him or herself and sits down pretty much every day to produce the written word. Some days it comes easy and others it comes hard. Some days it feels like you are creating a masterpiece and others it feels like you're spewing worthless garbage.

In the end, when the editing has been liberally applied, it is for the most part, consistent. The real joy for the true writer is in that emptiness where your whole being is called upon to produce. You know you have found the magic of creation when you find yourself caught up in a scene, look up and notice that two hours have suddenly passed and you have three pages of a first draft.

Aside from the discipline sitting down to write every day gives you, you have your storyline uppermost in your mind every day. The story threads are fresh, making it easier to pick up where you left off and begin the magic again. The constant attention your story gets gives it a continuity that stopping and starting disrupts. The end result is writing that has greater consistency.

There is a certain abandon that comes with the commitment that drops you down into an empty page. Jumping into that white space is the same as jumping off a cliff, not knowing where you are going to land, but having the faith that your whole mind, conscious and subconscious will focus their energies toward creating something from nothing.

Creating a reality. Yours.

Unleashing Your Imagination

A shaman's path is one of deep self-examination. For writers, the act of writing is also a process of self-examination. Writers constantly analyze themselves, the behaviors of others, and the world around them in an effort to understand who they are and the nature of the world they inhabit in order to find out what is important to them.

Where do your strongest feelings lie? What sets you off, fires you up, infuriates, intimidates, obsesses, or fascinates you? What do you love or hate with unbridled passion? Something in the newspaper, on the radio, or television get your blood pressure up? What grabbed your attention as a kid? Doctor Dolittle? King Arthur? Curious George? Dracula? Tarzan? Something by Heinlein, Bradbury, or Asimov? The thing that lurked in your closet or under your bed?

There lies the ore to be mined.

This is where you'll find the basis for your premise; the thesis that is the driving force behind your narrative. If it doesn't get you fired up, it's not worth writing about, because the lack of fire behind your convictions and fascinations will not inflame your writing with the passion necessary to drive your stories toward their inevitable conclusions.

If you find yourself struggling to find a theme that really matters to you on a deeper level, legendary science fiction wizard Ray Bradbury gave the following advice paraphrased here.

When you wake up in the morning, before you do anything else, go straight to your keyboard, pen and paper, or whatever else you compose your first drafts on, and write whatever comes to mind whether its dreams, snippets of random thought, impressions, or ideas, fresh out of sleep. Write a few paragraphs or pages of whatever comes out until the flow tapers off, then put those pages aside without reading them. Do this every morning for a few weeks, or until you have a good stack of pages, then read them straight through.

A theme will emerge.

Once you have your focus and sense of direction, scan the newspapers, libraries, and bookstores for anything and everything connected with your area of interest.

The field of anthropology is bursting with fascinating material that can enhance if not totally motivate any story. There are cultures in this world that are so alien from contemporary society that a writer could simply rename them and put them in another reality or another planet. Better still, bring in your imagination and let it run rampant, change physical details, take features from different cultures and mix or match them. You can even invent your own details.

Tied in with anthropology is history. Incredible things have happened in the life of this planet, both human induced and through natural forces. When two totally different cultures which have had no previous contact clash, each culture is shaken down to the very core of its system of beliefs.

Past events can be dramatized and recreated, both here and in other worlds or times, casting reality in a whole new light. Racism, war, revolution, discrimination, slavery, genocide, scientific breakthroughs, natural and unnatural disasters... The list is endless because it all comes down to the drama of unfolding lives and events and the change they bring, which is what fiction is all about.

Mythology is another vast playground of stories full of morals and observations of human foibles. Mythical beings, gods, worlds, and magic both benign and sinister are vehicles that embody ideas and philosophies. Any one of these can be altered, embellished, and tailored to fit your own ends.

Stephen King's **Salem's Lot** is a hugely successful retelling of the Dracula myth. In our "modern age", the bloodsucking vampire still has the power to fascinate, even mesmerize us. Ask Anne Rice and the huge following of her fans who have faithfully indulged in the chronicles of Lestat and Louis, or the dedicated fans of the **Twilight** series.

Can you imagine the equivalent of Pandora's Box on an alien planet and how the unleashing of a forbidden technology or cultural taboo could alter the fabric of your character's reality? If you have any doubts, study the lives of people like Galileo, da Vinci, and Einstein.

The world of science changes every day. Computer and electronic technology race ahead as do the fields of genetics and biology. Not only are they evolving, but they're merging, cross pollinating, and redefining each other. Numerous physical scientists have migrated from the world of quantum physics into the worlds of microbiology and genetics. Computer chips are being designed based on the architecture of the human brain.

Read, read, read! Aside from the obvious nonfiction research, read everything written in the fields that interest you. Find out what everyone else is doing. Which writers really grab you? Why?

Analyze them.

Get a feel for what's hot in the field and what's not. Maybe your idea is so novel, you'll create a whole new trend like cyberpunks, splatterpunks, steampunks, virtual realities, or worlds like that of J.R.R. Tolkien or J.K. Rowling, then people will be reading *your* work for inspiration and ideas.

Research what fascinates or affects you deeply, then write about it. It's all there waiting to be mined from the world around you and within you.

Training Your Brain -- Research

In the same way that a shaman prepares for a visionary, knowledge seeking journey, a writer must make their own plans. Before starting a new screenplay, or the long, grueling commitment of writing a novel, the writer needs sufficient material to sustain them for the duration of their story. The research portion of your project is the act of filling yourself with information in the same way you fill a large vessel.

The filling of your subconscious and the subsequent emptying is intrinsically tied in with the writing process. Once you gain insight into this mysterious event, you will have a better understanding of yourself and you will know and recognize the mental processes, thoughts, and feelings that go along with each stage of the journey.

There is the obvious danger of not doing enough research and there is the danger of getting over involved; one of the tricks the lazy, procrastinating part of your mind will use to keep you from sitting down in the chair and getting the job done. This diversionary tactic falls in the same category as house cleaning, dish washing, computer and video games, television, food, sex, drugs, and rock and roll.

There is a time and place to experience vices and virtues, but when they are used as escapes to keep you from sitting down and doing the work, you have to learn the signs and apply the necessary self-discipline. On the same note, there is also a philosophy of holding off on the fun stuff, using it as rewards and incentives.

When you do research, take in everything possible; film, video, audio, books, music, newspapers, magazines, pictures, lectures, and you're in a position to do so, visit the place where you're your tale. Think of it in terms of filling yourself. You have to your mind with all the ingredients you can until it's bursting at seams, then you want to hold off as long as possible to let the ew simmer. This part of the process is analogous to foreplay and lovemaking where each partner shows restraint, withholding the moment of fulfillment and letting the tension build for greater satisfaction.

The resulting "explosion" will propel your narrative forward with a strong enough push to carry it through the mid-book doldrums.

The key to this is learning to trust your subconscious by understanding how to train and feed it, trusting in the fact that it will deliver -- a*nd it will deliver*. When you learn what a mysterious ally your subconscious is, it will amaze you with what it brings to the party. You may find yourself in the middle of a scene, your logical mind feeling lost, when a line of thought, narrative, description, or dialogue will spring forth, sometimes faster than you can get it down. At these times, to hell with grammar, sentence structure, and everything else you've ever learned. Go with the flow and get it down. Making it perfect is what rewriting is all about.

There is a "no man's land" that lies between your opening lines and the end of your book, paragraph, sentence, or chapter, the place that Stephen King refers to as "falling into the page". You know where you want to go, but you have no idea how to get there. This is the point where your ally brings his powers to the endeavor. This is where the shaman takes flight.

It is also part of the process of "emptying out". Your subconscious will bring the right things at the right places at the right times. All you have to do is learn how to train it and trust it. The next thing you know, you have a page, a chapter, then a book. Though you did not consciously attempt every detail of it, you'll have the pleasant experience of discovering an underlying coherence in all you do. Ask any professional fiction writer how many times someone has come up to them and said: "I love the way you tied those pieces together and connected this to that. It was brilliant!" The writer will smile and nod, knowing full well they have no clue as to how he or she accomplished the lauded feat.

Once you have completed all of your research, how do you put it all together with any kind of coherence? One of the best ways is to put it into a flexible and by no means set in stone form known as an outline, but it is not the stale outline that comes to mind from the tortures of academia. It is a dynamic, shifting, developing, ever-forming entity.

Outlines

The very word brings fear and loathing to the hearts of the uninitiated because of the negative conditioning forced on us by the academic establishment. Many professionals swear against outlines, and insist on "winging it" without one, but chances are they either have the ability to organize the information in their minds, or they use what has been called a "cluster outline", which is essentially a mass of ideas circled and connected by lines.

Regardless of the philosophy, outlines are useful organizational tools that give coherence, structure, and focus to your work, providing a skeleton and a map that are essential for a tight, well-constructed story.

An outline provides an organized structure of your thoughts that follow a set of rules that define it as a story. If you do not follow the rules, it will not be a story.

A word about rules.

There are none.

In the beginning it seems like all you hear about are rules. Point of view, tense, scene setting, characterization, description, show don't tell, etc., yet in essence, there are no hard and fast rules. What there is, is technique, innovation, and above all *structure*.

Once you learn what are considered "rules", you can transform rules into tools and the more you utilize them, the more liberating they become. There is not one single story telling problem that cannot be solved by being creative in your use of proven fiction writing techniques.

The whole breadth, texture, and interweaving of the tapestry that ties a story together makes it like a giant puzzle, except you get to craft your own pieces. This is the part -- *the big picture*, where an outline can be invaluable.

Initially it can be nothing more than the mass of your ideas and research all put together, written in free flowing, stream of consciousness. It doesn't have to be highly detailed and the ideas do not have to be fully formed. If there's a scene bubbling around in your head that's dying to get on the page, condense it down to a key phrase, a snatch of dialogue, or a brief description. Think of this snippet as a tab on a file in your mind that will produce the whole file when you pull up on it.

Hold off on the actual writing until the time comes to allow your subconscious to do what it does best. Give it time to cook. More often than not, your subconscious will toss up bits and pieces of what it's cooking. Take the tidbits, go back to your outline and jot them down, adding meat to your scenes.

When you have all your ideas accumulated in one place, you should have around ten to twenty pages. Go through it once or twice, adding details where you feel the need, then give it a rest.

Anywhere from a couple of hours to a day or a week will do. Whatever feels best to you. When you can't hold yourself back any longer, pick it up again and give it a look from the standpoint of *dramatic structure*. What is the best way to present your information?

Continue working at it however many times you feel is necessary, refining what you have until you're comfortable with it and you'll have a *working outline*. One that is not set in stone. It will be the map to keep you heading in the direction that you want to go.

At this point you may not have a clear vision of the ending, or for that matter, the details of the scenes that make up the middle. That's part of keeping everything flexible. The more pages you get under your belt doing the actual writing, the more you will change your working outline.

As you progress in the writing, your outline will continue to change with the knowledge that accumulates as you go. By the time you reach the end, the finished product will have no semblance to what you started with. Your story, characters, situations, and relationships will unfold, growing and developing with a life of their own, like leaves and branches on a tree.

Everything Is Energy And That's All There Is To It

"Everything is energy and that's all there is to it. Match the frequency of the reality you want and you cannot help but get that reality. It can be no other way. This is not philosophy. This is physics."

This popular quotation is often attributed to Albert Einstein, but is widely believed to come from a channeler named Darryl Anka who assigned the words to an entity named Bashar.

Nonetheless, as a writer, if you can create the frequency of the reality you want with your words, you cannot help but create that reality in the hearts and minds of your readers.

Einstein did speak about the relationship between matter and energy in a 1948 film called "Atomic Physics", where he stated, *"It followed from the special theory of relativity that mass and energy are both but different manifestations of the same thing — a somewhat unfamiliar conception for the average mind."*

In other words, according to Einstein everything *is* energy, and in the world view of a shaman *everything* without question is energy whether it be waking reality, dreams, visions, solid objects, emotions, sights, sounds, smells, or any other sensations. Indigenous shamans do not separate dreaming, waking, or visionary worlds. To them it is all one continuum, and each realm carries just as much weight and validity as the other. For them everything is connected in one interactive whole. Modern day quantum physicists have also embraced this as a result of two principles they have learned through the close scientific observation of energetic principles in action.

The first is non-locality or action at a distance, the direct interaction of two objects that are separated in space with no perceivable intermediate agency or mechanism. Quantum non-locality refers to what Einstein called the "spooky action at a distance" of quantum entanglement, a physical phenomenon that occurs when pairs or groups of particles are generated or interact in ways where the quantum state of each particle cannot be described independently. Instead, a quantum state is given for the system as a whole, which proves that everything is connected to everything else, whether seen or unseen.

The second principle is that of a hologram which we know of as a photographic picture composed of a great number of small parts, all of which contain the picture as a whole. When a hologram is broken into many pieces, what remains is many small but complete pictures of the whole. The ocean provides another example of a holographic reality.

Since the ocean is made up of water, we can say that the ocean is contained in every drop. Similarly, a ray of the Sun contains the Sun itself, and in a seed, the entire structure of the tree is contained within it. Additionally, every cell of our body contains the complete information about the entire mind-body system. Each of the 100 billion cells that make up the body contains the complete version of the original DNA which was the source of the entire body.

All levels of creation are analogous to each other because each level of creation is an expression of the whole, interpreted through a different vibratory lens.

Each distinctive character that a writer creates in the wholeness of the universe that they bring into existence is indeed an expression of the whole, interpreted through a different vibratory lens. This constitutes their unique point of view.

What is vibration?

Energy.

What is of primary importance in bringing a story to life is energy. Without it there is no sign of life, and in truth without it there is *no* life.

The author of the world being created makes them the God or Goddess of that world, which gives them complete control over time, space, and every detail that lies within them. Every single thing within this interconnected created reality is made of energy.

For a shaman to become a master of reality they must follow what is called the power path which amounts to becoming a master of energy. This is what a writer must do to be the master of the worlds that they create and the tools that they have at their disposal to accomplish this are words, phrases, and sentences as well as a multitude of other related elements.

The word *energy* derives from the Ancient Greek: ἐνέργεια *energeia* "activity, operation", which is believed to appear for the first time in the work of Aristotle. In contrast to the modern definition, energeia was a qualitative philosophical concept, broad enough to include ideas such as happiness and pleasure. Every emotion that we feel, we experience as a different kind of energy, each with its own unique qualities.

In physics, energy is a property of objects, transferable among them via fundamental interactions, which can be converted in form but not created or destroyed. Energy transformation or energy conversion is the process of changing one form of energy to another which is what happens to the shaman in his journey to the underworld where he is dismembered and reborn anew by facing his deepest fears.

This is also what happens to the protagonist when he undergoes the ultimate ordeal that makes him into the hero whether it is Frodo facing off against Gollum on the precipice of the fires of Mt. Doom in Mordor, Harry Potter facing off against Voldemort, or Luke Skywalker going up against the Death Star, relying only on The Force.

In order to understand the forces at work in these complex processes, it is best to start with the basics of energy and the qualities that it possesses to form a basis for expanding the myriad relationships that make up a comprehensive narrative whether applying it to short stories, novels, or screenplays.

Energy indicates movement and movement denotes transformation. If you start with the concept of a point, a point has no dimension and it is static and unmoving. If you extend that point in one direction, you have a line. The more energy that is put out to overcome inertia, the further that point moves and the longer the line becomes, so a longer line is a sign of more expended energy.

The distance between these two points contain the potential, which in the study of electricity is called voltage, electrical potential difference, electric tension or electric pressure -- the electric potential difference between two points, or the difference in electric potential energy of a unit charge transported between two points.

Implicit in the difference between two points is the concept of polarity which is denoted by two poles labeled positive and negative. Batteries, fuel cells and solar cells all produce this direct current, known as DC. The terminals of a battery are always, respectively, positive and negative and current always flows in the same direction between those two terminals.

The power that comes from a power plant on the other hand is called alternating current, known as AC where the direction of the current reverses or alternates 60 times per second in the U.S. or 50 times per second in Europe.

There are two characteristic of alternating current that come into play when this concept of movement is applied to the plotting, structure, and interaction of all the elements that make up a story. These are known as amplitude and frequency.

The greater the amplitude of a wave, the higher the level of energy that it carries. With a sound wave, this means that the sound will be louder. With light, the bigger the amplitude means the light will be brighter. In water, the bigger the amplitude of the waves, the higher they will be. In drama, this indicates the level of intensity of the event.

Frequency is the number of occurrences of a repeating event per unit time.

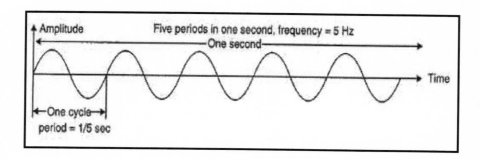

How these two characteristics of the movement of energy are manipulated dictate the plotting, pacing, and structure of a story. These elements can be seen in their most basic form in the classic three act structure where amplitude is shown as intensity and frequency is shown as time. As the plot unfolds in a three act structure, each consecutive act rises higher than the one preceding it until it reaches its climax.

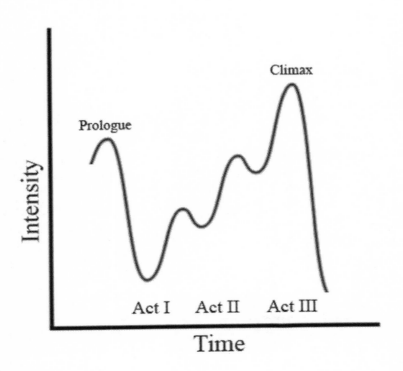

Beginnings

Y ou'd better hook them right away.
Grab your readers with the first word and don't let go.
It has to be your very best writing.

If you've spent any time studying dramatic writing you've heard these admonitions at one time or another. If you haven't you will, until they become the clichés that they are. They became clichés for a very good reason. You have to do everything in your power to stand out above the rest.

Invariably, newer writers get caught like the proverbial deer in the headlights, worrying about blocks of back story told in line after line of narrative. The key word here is *told* as opposed to *shown*, which is also known as reader feeder. Nowhere else is this more prevalent than in beginnings where newer writers do it the most. Real beginners often do it throughout the whole manuscript.

That can't be, beginners say. You have to know about my main character's twenty-seven years in the Shaolin temple, so when he kicks the bad guy between the eyes in the first action scene, he's believable. Wrong. Don't worry about back story. If the scene or the information is that important it can be done in a flashback, in dialogue, a note, letter, book, newspaper, on the deathbed -- basically wherever it fits in with the *maximum dramatic impact*.

A wise writer once said "information is the enemy of drama". If you take nothing else from this book, take that little gem. Instead of bogging down your lift-off with chunks of back story that tell, but do not show, hold back as much information as you can in the same way you would give someone the first clue of a puzzle. Done with the right finesse, holding back will create more questions in your reader's mind, giving them another reason to keep turning the pages to find out who, what, when, where, or why.

In order to keep your unfolding plot rushing forward, headlong, with a fast rising conflict that gives your narrative an impending sense of an inevitable climax that comes to a resolution and begins the cycle again, active verbs, action, dialogue, and descriptions should all be streamlined in each sentence while eliminating unnecessary adjectives, adverbs, and passive voice.

Every narrative word and every spoken word should move the plot forward, create conflict, and reveal character. From word one, it needs to creep up the roller coaster track toward the first heart-dropping fall while letting the characters reveal who they are by what they say, do, and think.

Your opening scene should orient your readers in the world that you have created and give them a solid sample of what's to come by setting the pace and lay down the groundwork for the events that follow. If possible, the opening should be a microcosm of the whole story, giving your readers the start of the major conflict. If it's a science fiction story, it should have all the setting, elements and atmosphere of the world you're creating, so the reader knows from the beginning what kind of a tale they're in for. If it's a romance, maybe you want to put in the first blush of attraction, or in the case of many love stories, the first repulsion. A mystery might open with a murder, or at the very least a crime that is the inciting incident that leads to one.

If it's an event from another time, place, or point of view that triggers things in "present time," meaning the time and place in which your story unfolds, you can do it as a prologue, making your opening a kind of "set piece". The important thing is to set your reader up for what is to come, giving them enough details to tantalize them into reading more without giving too much away.

A Latin term that describes how a story should open is *in media res* which means in the middle of the action. Dive right in, opening with a line of dialogue or action in the middle of an event that is already happening. There's no need to explain why the six-foot-seven gorilla is pointing an Uzi in your protagonist's face. Properly written, the scene will be so riveting, the reader won't care what happened before, or how your protagonist got there. They'll be too wrapped up in *what's going to happen next.*

Take some time, pick up your favorite writers and read their openings. See how they set the hook with an eye to what works. Which ones grab you? Which ones don't? Why?

Cast out your line and set the hook. Grab your reader by the throat and drag them into your landscape without letting go until the bitter end. Don't worry about the back story and all the non-dramatic information you feel the reader needs to know.

You can hook your audience more by what you don't tell them.

Motivation

In the beginning was the word and the word was *motivation*, which is the embodiment of yearning, desire, and hunger. It is the essence of life. Passion. At the core of it all, before there is a plot, a story, or a character, there is the primal driving energy that drives your characters forward toward their destinies which lie in wait for them at the climax of your story. Everything your creations say, do, and think is propelled by this driving force that brings them to a moment of truth. Their every thought and actions are dictated by it.

It is their very reason for being.

Once motivation is established, you have to know it intimately for every one of your creations, then you have to insure that your readers know it, yet you can't be too blatant revealing it unless it is a peak moment and it comes as an answer to a mystery. It is far better to hint at it, revealing it slowly as your characters *develop*. A snatch of dialogue here, an action there. A thought.

What does it tell you about a person and their motivations when they say one thing and do the opposite?

In real life, motivation is often intangible. You can watch and listen to what people say and do and make your own deductions, but there is never any way to be absolutely sure. The only thing you can be absolutely sure of is your own motivation, and even that can be questionable at times.

As a fiction writer, you have the luxury of dictating your character's thoughts which allows you to direct and guide them. Their every thought and action are controlled by an unseen will. Yours.

You have to motivate them. Without strong and well documented motivation, your story and creations will have no life. No driving force. No spark burning inside them that keeps them alive.

A shaman abandons himself to the powers that he cultivates and true artists give themselves to their work. Your will is what motivates your characters. The act of putting your will into your creations is a way you put yourself into your work. This is what makes it live and breathe and what makes it real and vital. This is the breath of life creators give to their creations.

Aside from the motivations of your secondary characters, there is the main driving force that propels the story itself. In the study of fiction writing, the word *motivation* and the word *thesis* are synonymous. What drives your main character? Everything hangs on this.

Like the life inside of us and the death that waits for us in the "real world", motivation is the spark of your divine will that gives your fictional reality the impetus to move forward toward its inevitable conclusion. Solid motivation equals a solid gripping story that a reader will not want to put down.

That is the object of the whole exercise.

The Hero's Journey

The origins of The Hero's Journey has its roots in the ancient rituals of shamanic initiation. Joseph Campbell, one of the greatest mythologists of all time summarized the steps of the Hero's Journey in his seminal work, ***The Hero with a Thousand Faces***. Author Christopher Vogler, explored these themes in his popular work, ***The Writer's Journey: Mythic Structure For Writers***.

These works made a major impact on writing and story-telling. Filmmakers like Steven Spielberg, George Lucas, and Francis Coppola owe their successes in part to the ageless patterns of the shaman's journey and path to power that Joseph Campbell has identified. Popular cultural heroes like Harry Potter, Bilbo and Frodo Baggins, Batman, Superman, Luke Skywalker and many others all follow the Hero's Journey.

All story-telling, consciously or not, follows the ancient patterns of myth, and all stories can be understood in terms of the hero myth, which has its roots in shamanism, which occurs in every culture, in every time, and is as infinitely varied as the human race itself. Stories built on the model of the hero myth have an appeal that is felt by everyone, because they spring from a universal source in the collective unconscious, and reflect universal concerns by dealing with the child-like but universal questions.

Who am I?

Where did I come from?

Where will I go when I die?

What is good and what is evil?

What should I do about it?

What will tomorrow be like?

Where did yesterday go?

Is there anybody else out there?

In his book, ***The Writer's Journey: Mythic Structure For Writers*** Christopher Vogler gave a condensed version of the hero myth and amended it to reflect common themes in movies. What follows is Vogler's amended version with additional comments.

THE STAGES OF THE HERO'S JOURNEY

1.) ORDINARY WORLD

Most stories take us to a special world that is new and alien to its hero. If you're going to tell a story about a fish out of his customary element, you have to create a contrast by showing him in his mundane, ordinary world. In the Harrison Ford film, WITNESS you see both the Amish boy and the policeman in their ordinary worlds before they are thrust into alien worlds – the farm boy into the city, and the city cop into the unfamiliar countryside. In STAR WARS you see Luke Skywalker being bored to death as a farm boy before he tackles the universe. This is the original place of balance that gets upset and starts the hero on their quest to "reset the balance".

This is the place of normal everyday life where the would be shaman finds themselves prior to "the call".

2.) CALL TO ADVENTURE

Here the hero is presented with a problem, challenge or adventure. Maybe the land is dying, as in the King Arthur stories about the search for the Grail. In STAR WARS, it's Princess Leia's holographic message to Obi Wan Kenobi, who then asks Luke to join the quest. In detective stories, it's the hero being offered a new case. In romantic comedies it could be the first sight of that special but annoying someone the hero or heroine will be pursuing/sparring with.

In shamanism, it is the first sign from the supernatural that touches them in some way. Shamans can be chosen by odd behaviors or predilections, being struck by lightning and surviving, by interactions with particular plants and animals, by great sickness, fever dreams, visions or some other physiological or psychological crisis.

3.) REFUSAL OF THE CALL

Often at this point the hero balks at the threshold of adventure. He or she is facing the greatest of all fears – fear of the unknown. At this point Luke refuses Obi Wan's call to adventure, and returns to his aunt and uncle's farmhouse, only to find they have been barbecued by the Emperor's storm troopers. Suddenly Luke is no longer reluctant, and is eager to undertake the adventure. He is motivated.

At this point the shaman to be struggles with their condition and/or status which makes them uncomfortable and out of place in their old world, yet in fear of the unknown new reality that has come knocking. They walk in a gray area between the worlds, with one foot in the old, and one in the new. Neither of them feels right.

4.) MEETING WITH THE MENTOR

By this time a story will introduce a Merlin-like character who is the hero's mentor. In THE HOBBIT and THE LORD OF THE RINGS it is Gandalf the Wizard. In HARRY POTTER we have another literal wizard in Dumbledore. The mentor gives advice and sometimes magical weapons. This is what Obi Wan does when he gives Luke his father's light saber.

The mentor can go so far with the hero, but eventually the hero must face the unknown by himself. Sometimes the Wise Old Man/Woman is required to give the hero a swift kick in the pants to get the adventure going.

In traditional indigenous societies the only person someone can turn to for help in overcoming a physical, psychological, spiritual crisis is the shaman whose archetype is clearly seen in the wizard, Jedi knight, or sage.

5.) CROSSING THE THRESHOLD

The hero fully enters the special world of the story for the first time. This is the moment where the story takes off and the adventure gets going. The balloon goes up, the romance begins, the spaceship blasts off, the wagon train gets rolling. Dorothy sets out on the Yellow Brick Road. The hero is now committed to his/her journey and there's no turning back.

This is the point where the shaman/acolyte ingests their first visionary plants and/or embarks on their first vision quest. This act sets them off, isolates them, and singles them out from the rest of their society and puts them in an altered state where the normal rules of life and society no longer apply.

It is the first step into the unknown.

6.) TESTS, ALLIES, ENEMIES

The hero is forced to make allies and enemies in the special world, and must pass certain tests and challenges that are part of his/her training. In STAR WARS the cantina is the setting for the forging of an important alliance with Han Solo and the start of an important enmity with Jabba the Hutt. In CASABLANCA Rick's Café is the setting for the "alliances and enmities" phase and in many Westerns it's the saloon where these relationships are tested.

When the shaman's altered state begins, this is where he encounters his shadow, which can include allies and guides like power animals, power plants, and elemental spirits, as well as dark, sinister forces from the underworld that challenge him by raising and manifesting his deepest fears.

7.) APPROACH TO THE INMOST CAVE

The hero comes at last to a dangerous place, often deep underground, where the object of the quest is hidden. In the Arthurian stories the Chapel Perilous is the dangerous chamber where the seeker finds the Grail. In many myths the hero has to descend into hell to retrieve a loved one, or into a cave to fight a dragon and gain a treasure. It's Theseus going to the Labyrinth to face the Minotaur. In STAR WARS it's Luke and company being sucked into the Death Star where they will rescue Princess Leia. Sometimes it's just the hero going into his/her own dream world to confront fears and overcome them.

This is the shaman's entry to the crucible where the fires of transformation will destroy the old ego-based paradigms; the jaguar's lair where a huge all-encompassing maw of mortal fear and darkness await. It is the chrysalis where the formless remains of what is no longer relevant awaits its fate.

8.) SUPREME ORDEAL

This is the moment where the hero touches bottom. He/she faces the possibility of death, brought to the brink in a fight with a mythical beast. For us, the audience standing outside the cave waiting for the victor to emerge, it's a black moment. In STAR WARS, it's the harrowing moment in the bowels of the Death Star, where Luke, Leia and company are trapped in the giant trash-masher. Luke is pulled under by the tentacled monster that lives in the sewage and is held down so long that the audience begins to wonder if he's dead. IN E.T., THE EXTRATERRESTRIAL, E. T. momentarily appears to die on the operating table.

This is a critical moment in any story, an ordeal where the hero appears to die and be born again. It's a major source of the magic of the hero myth. At this point the audience has been led to identify with the hero and are encouraged to experience the brink-of-death feeling with the hero. The audience are temporarily depressed, and then revived by the hero's return from death.

This is the magic of any well-designed amusement park thrill ride. Space Mountain or the Great White knuckler make the passengers feel like they're going to die. There's a great thrill that comes with surviving a moment like that.

This is the moment of transformation where the shamanic initiate surrenders the ego and every other aspect of their being to forces greater than him or herself. This is the literal "moment of truth" where they taste death and experience resurrection. You're never more alive than when you think you're going to die.

9.) SEIZING THE SWORD, REWARD

Having survived death, beaten the dragon, slain the Minotaur, the hero now takes possession of the treasure they have come seeking. Sometimes it's a special weapon like a magic sword, a token like the Grail, or some elixir which can heal the wounded land.

The hero may settle a conflict with his father or with his shadowy nemesis. In RETURN OF THE JEDI, Luke is reconciled with both, as he discovers that the dying Darth Vader is his father, and not such a bad guy after all.

The hero may also be reconciled with a woman. Often she is the treasure he's come to win or rescue, and there is often a love scene or sacred marriage at this point. Women in these stories (or men if the hero is female) tend to be shape-shifters who appear to change in form or age, reflecting the confusing and constantly changing aspects of the opposite sex as seen from the hero's point of view. The hero's supreme ordeal may grant him a better understanding of women, leading to a reconciliation with the opposite sex.

At this point, the shaman accepts and embraces their shadow self and begins to integrate both the positive and negative including their fears, insecurities, and numerous other repressed or denied aspects of themselves. In Jungian terms this represents individuation.

10.) THE ROAD BACK.

The hero is not out of the woods yet. Some of the best chase scenes come at this point, as the hero is pursued by the vengeful forces from whom he has stolen the elixir or the treasure. This is the chase as Luke and friends escape from the Death Star with Princess Leia and the plans that will bring down Darth Vader.

If the hero has not yet managed to reconcile with his father or the gods, they may come raging after him at this point. This is the moonlight bicycle flight of Elliott and E. T. as they escape from "Keys" (Peter Coyote), a force representing governmental authority. By the end of the movie Keys and Elliott have been reconciled and it even looks like Keys will end up as Elliott's step-father.

In the shaman's world, this is where all of the scattered pieces of the ego, spirit, and essence are reintegrated in a new way with a world view that is completely different from the old one. This new "enlightened" perspective is enhanced as a result of the fear embracing act of transformation and imbued with the personal power and knowledge that the shaman has earned by accepting and acknowledging his shadow.

11.) RESURRECTION

The hero emerges from the special world, transformed by his/her experience. There is often a replay here of the mock death-and-rebirth of Stage 8, as the hero once again faces death and survives. The Star Wars movies play with this theme constantly – all three of the original films feature a final battle scene in which Luke is almost killed, appears to be dead for a moment, and then miraculously survives, transformed into a new being by his experience.

Here the shaman returns as a man or woman of power. As part of the initiation, this transformed being is challenged anew by the negative antagonistic forces that started their quest to reset the balance. In this confrontation they overcome their opposition, empowered by their new found power and knowledge, proving to themselves and subsequently to the world that they have won out over the forces of darkness.

12.) RETURN WITH THE ELIXIR

The hero comes back to the ordinary world, but the adventure would be meaningless unless he/she brought back the elixir, treasure, or some lesson from the special world. Sometimes it's just knowledge or experience, but he must come back with the elixir or some boon to mankind, or he's doomed to repeat the adventure until he does. Many comedies use this ending, as a foolish character refuses to learn his lesson and embarks on the same folly that got him in trouble in the first place.

Sometimes the boon is treasure won on the quest, or love, or just the knowledge that the special world exists and can be survived. Sometimes it's simply coming home with a good story to tell.

This is the reason that shamans are referred to as bridges. Their task is to travel the realms of spirit and visit other dimensions and realities that are incomprehensible to the uninitiated and return with the knowledge and wisdom gained there to benefit and heal those in need.

Plato's "Parable of the Cave" provides a great metaphor for the gap in perception that a shaman/hero must bridge to share the "elixir".

Plato has Socrates describe a gathering of people who have lived chained to the wall of a cave all of their lives, facing a blank wall. The people watch shadows projected on the wall by things passing in front of a fire behind them, and begin to designate names to these shadows. The shadows are as close as the prisoners get to viewing reality. He then explains how the philosopher (shaman/hero) is like a prisoner who is freed from the cave and comes to understand that the shadows on the wall do not make up reality at all, as he can perceive the true form of reality rather than the mere shadows seen by the prisoners.

His attempts to articulate this new found expanded view of reality is incomprehensible to those still chained to the wall as they have no precedent to gauge it by, so he must strive to "bridge the worlds" in whatever way he can to share the wisdom that he has risked everything to learn on his adventure outside the bounds of what is known.

In summary: The hero is introduced in his ORDINARY WORLD where he receives the CALL TO ADVENTURE. He is RELUCTANT at first to CROSS THE FIRST THRESHOLD where he eventually encounters TESTS, ALLIES and ENEMIES. He reaches the INNERMOST CAVE where he endures the SUPREME ORDEAL. He SEIZES THE SWORD or the treasure and is pursued on the ROAD BACK to his world. He is RESURRECTED and transformed by his experience. He RETURNS to his ordinary world with a treasure, boon, or ELIXIR to benefit his world.

From Vogler's *"The Writer's Journey: Mythic Structure For Writers"*

THE HERO'S JOURNEY

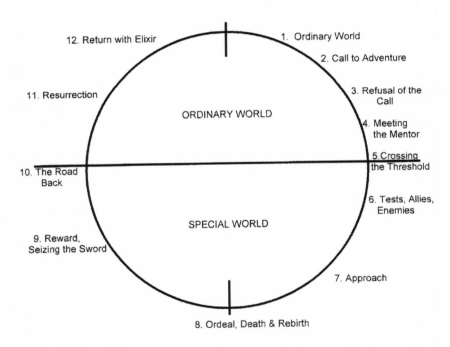

The Moving Crucible

The definition of a story is conflict and it should be advanced with every word, phrase, sentence, paragraph, and calculated punctuation. Everything should flow toward rising conflict that sparks a confrontation and an explosion which either brings the story to its conclusion, or leaves things flying headlong toward a still bigger conflict that comes to a conclusion or leads to an even bigger clash. This is the rhythm. This is the pace. This is the heartbeat of storytelling.

Up and down, back and forth, dark and light; the dance of two polarities, each dependent on the other, shifting frequency and amplitude according to the plotting and pacing of the story. There can be no light without darkness to set it off against. Up cannot exist without down. A wise martial arts master, grasping at the essence of confrontation said it succinctly with the simple words, "No opponent, no game."

Fiction is about relationships, good, bad, and all the rest. The more at cross-purposes the main players in the story are, the better the story. Characters in conflict is what creates character development. You never know a person's true mettle until you see them in confrontation, preferably backed into a corner.

There are many truths about storytelling. One of the most profound and central is the fact that *character is revealed through conflict.* If there's conflict, your characters will unfold, showing themselves, their fears, passions, and intentions when they have it all on the line.

Your story should unfold in an inevitable, forward flowing,

burgeoning progression which arises as the only possible outcome of two opposites coming together, each trying to achieve its own purpose, each standing in the way of the other.

A story begins with conflict. The greater the conflict, the greater the polarity in forces, which translates into more energy. This concentration of energy is the crucible of transformation and the opening of the story is analogous to lighting a fuse. The fiery spark that travels along the length of the fuse can be called "the story moment", which is the point where your reader or audience is focused during the course of the unfolding narative. This story moment can be compared to the word that lights up when a karaoke player highlights the moment of the song that is being sung and emphasized. It should contain all of the energy of that moment that holds the greatest potential.

Examining the roots of the words used to characterize these forces helps to define the energies at work within this crucible.
The basis of the words protagonist and antagonist come from **agonist,** which is a chemical that binds to a receptor, activating it to produce a biological response. An agonist causes an action, and an antagonist blocks the action of the agonist. To put it more simply an agonist is something that initiates a response.

Thesis and antithesis come from the noun **synthesis,** which refers to a combination of two or more entities that together form something new. The corresponding verb, **synthesize** means *to make or form a synthesis.* This is the essence of transformation.

The Story Moment

In literary, metaphorical, psychological, and shamanic terms, the antagonist represents the protagonist's shadow.

When a shaman descends into the underworld to undergo transformation by dismemberment, or in South American Indian traditions to be, "swallowed by the jaguar", he is in effect being swallowed by his shadow, which is the equivalent of psychological dismemberment, or the "ordeal, death, and rebirth" of the hero in The Hero's Journey. In shamanic lore it is a bid for power, and power is the reward for surviving this terrifying encounter, characterized in The Hero's Journey by the "seizing of the sword".

In Jungian psychology, the shadow refers to an unconscious aspect of the personality that the conscious ego does not identify in itself. Because most people tend to reject or remain ignorant of the least desirable aspects of their personalities, the shadow is largely negative. To put it another way, it is everything that a person is not fully conscious of. There are also positive aspects which can remain hidden in one's shadow.

"Everyone carries a shadow," Jung wrote, "and the less it is embodied in the individual's conscious life, the blacker and denser it is." It includes our link to more primitive animal instincts which are superseded during early childhood by the conscious mind.

This is the darkness of the unknown that we fear at the deepest instinctual depths of our being; the hero's greatest fears that he or she must overcome to seize the sword, retrieve the holy grail, or claim their personal power so they can return home triumphant and restore the balance that was lost in a new (transformed) way.

According to Jung, the shadow, being instinctive and irrational, is prone to psychological projection in which a perceived personal inferiority is recognized as a perceived moral deficiency in someone else. Jung writes that if these projections remain hidden, "The projection-making factor (the Shadow archetype) then has a free hand and can realize its object--if it has one--or bring about some other situation characteristic of its power." These projections insulate and harm individuals by acting as a constantly thickening veil of illusion between the ego and the real world.

As mentioned, the shadow can also harbor positive aspects which can remain hidden within it, but they can be revealed in the projections of the hero made evident in what can be called the character universe, which will be explored in more detail.

In shamanism and in the more revealing and sometimes fantastical parts of the Hero's Journey, the shadow may appear in dreams, visions, and various other forms, including human. Its appearance and role depend greatly on the living experience of the individual, because much of the shadow develops in the individual's mind rather than simply being inherited in the collective unconscious. Some Jungians maintain that '*The shadow* contains, besides the personal shadow, the shadow of society, fed by the neglected and repressed collective values'.

Jung also made the suggestion of more than one layer making up the shadow. The top layers contain the meaningful flow and manifestations of direct personal experiences. These are made unconscious in the individual by such things as the change of attention from one thing to another, simple forgetfulness, or repression. Underneath these idiosyncratic layers are the archetypes that form the psychic contents of all human experiences. Jung described this deeper layer as "a psychic activity which goes on independently of the conscious mind and is not dependent even on the upper layers of the unconscious—untouched, and perhaps untouchable by personal experience." This bottom layer of the shadow is what Jung referred to as the collective unconscious.

The encounter with the shadow plays a central part in the process of synthesis and transformation within the crucible. Jung termed this process individuation and stated that the course of individuation exhibits a certain formal regularity. Its signposts and milestones are various archetypal symbols' marking its stages; and of these 'the first stage leads to the experience of the SHADOW'.

"The shadow personifies everything that the subject refuses to acknowledge about himself" and represents "a tight passage, a narrow door, whose painful constriction no one is spared who goes down to the deep well". This tight passage is in fact the birth canal that must be passed through, "the road back" in the Hero's Journey that leads to "Resurrection", which is rebirth coming from the death of the ego.

The dissolution of the persona and the launch of the individuation process also brings with it the danger of falling victim to the shadow, the black shadow that everybody carries with him, the inferior and hidden aspect of the personality. In Obi-Wan-Kenobi's vernacular, this is the dark side of the force.

According to Jung, the shadow sometimes overwhelms a person's actions; for example, when the conscious mind is shocked, confused, or paralyzed by indecision. 'A man who is possessed by his shadow is always standing in his own light and falling into his own traps ... living below his own level': hence, in terms of the story of Dr. Jekyll and Mr. Hyde, 'it must be Jekyll, the conscious personality, who integrates the shadow, and *not* vice versa. Otherwise the conscious becomes the slave of the autonomous shadow'.

On the road home, the hero or shaman travels back through the healing spirals. Here the struggle is to retain *awareness* of the shadow, but not identification with it. 'Non-identification demands considerable moral effort and prevents a descent into that darkness. Though the conscious mind is liable to be submerged at any moment in the unconscious, understanding acts like a life-saver by integrating the unconscious and reincorporating the shadow into the personality, producing a stronger, wider consciousness than before, which in shamanism is referred to as personal power, demonstrated by the metaphor of ***Plato's Parable of the Cave***.

The Heart of the Matter

The Temple of Anthropocosmic Man at Luxor is a masterpiece of art, science, and spirituality laid out in an elegant structure that is architecturally rendered to exhibit within its design and artwork the same proportions as the proportions of Man, as well as the mathematical and geometrical structure of the Cosmos and its locale within human consciousness. Pharaonic Consciousness not only recognized Man as the center of the Universe, it could formally equate it as well.

This ancient depiction of a holographic world view in which the microcosm is in the macrocosm so clearly demonstrated in the Temple of Anthropocosmic Man is a shamanic belief that infuses the shaman's transformation and subsequently The Hero's Journey. The design and layout of the temple and its meaning provide the framework for what can be called the character universe.

In this model, the heart, which can be considered the giver of life, is located at the center of man. It gives life to and supports all the other organs surrounding it in the same way that the sun at the center of our solar system gives life to and supports all of the planets surrounding it. Each planet that orbits this solar furnace which is the crucible of the heart has historically been attributed with its own personality. Mars has been called "The God of War", Venus "The Goddess of Beauty and Love". The others have their own unique attributes, or to put it another way, their own unique energies.

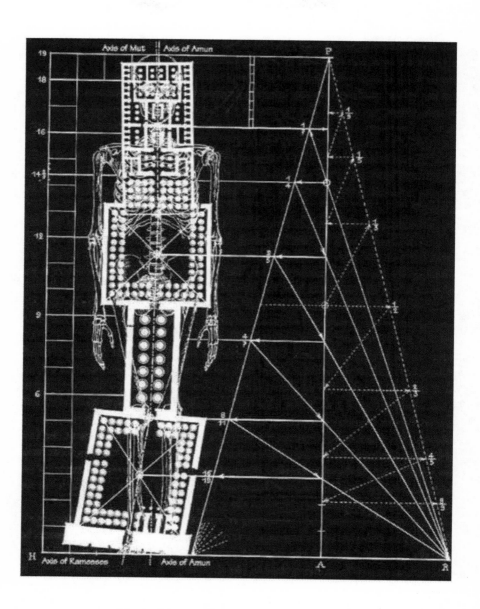

The Temple of Anthropocosmic Man

Centuries before it became a pop culture fad, Astrology was a highly respected science which was an integral part of Astronomy. In addition to the Earth and the seasonal signs of the zodiac, Astrology deals with ten planets, namely the Sun, the Moon (the two luminaries are considered planets in astrology), Mercury, Venus, Mars, Jupiter, Saturn, Uranus, Neptune and Pluto. Each planet has its precise function in the natal chart, and represents a specific energy. The planet's action is influenced by the sign it tenants and plays out primarily in the area of life indicated by the house where it is posited.

In shamanism, the heart in man is the sun of his personal cosmos which is connected to the sun, which is the giver of life in our solar system, especially on planet earth. This sun in turn is connected to a bigger sun, which is connected to a bigger sun, infinitely, all the way back to Source.

An old adage in shamanism, made popular by Carlos Castaneda attributed to Don Juan, the Yaqui shaman, is that, "A warrior must follow a path with heart." In other words, follow your heart. If it takes you back to Source, then you have found your way home.

In the same way that the sun at the center of our solar system is influenced by and influences the planets in its orbit, so do the organs and their energies in the human body interact with its heart.

Your protagonist is the heart of the universe that you are creating. Like the planets, all of the secondary characters in your story are energetic influences that represent different aspects of your protagonist that manifest different sides of his or her personality. The supporting allies of the protagonist mirror and support the good, including positive aspects of the shadow and the antagonistic ones reflect the darker side.

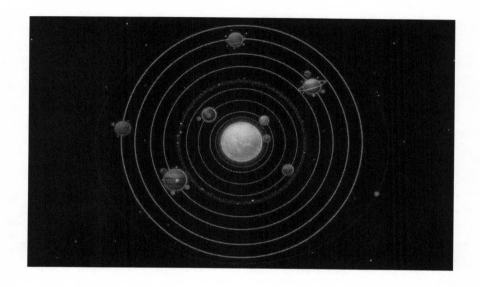

The Solar System

Shamanic Mirroring and the Wizard of Oz

The supporting characters in a story mirror the different aspects and sub-personalities of the protagonist, providing them with reflections of their inner world. The outer world is a reflection of the inner, much of which is shadow, good and bad. Some of the reflections can be beautiful, but many are undesirable and denied. It is said that when certain people in our lives annoy us, it is because they reflect a shadow part of ourselves that we deny, so not only do they reflect what is inside of us back to us, but we project the unwanted parts onto them to avoid seeing it in ourselves.

Character reveals itself through conflict on multiple levels that encompass inner and outer worlds. This circular diagram from Robert McKee's *Story* provides an excellent map of the zones of conflict. Any zone can interact with any other zone in any number of ways, providing ample opportunity to discover complex characters and complex relationships.

From *Robert McKee's "Story"*

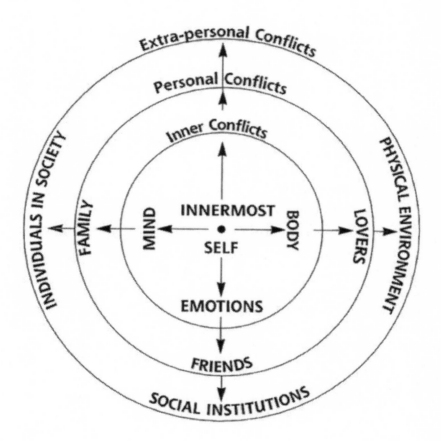

You can also see this as the "center of the universe" as it maps the protagonist and the interplay of energetic interactions that start in the middle and work their way out. At the center of the universe we find the innermost self which is composed of mind, body, and emotions. Everyone knows what it is like to have conflict between these three forces. Typically, one of them leads while the other two are relegated to shadow until a strong stimulus causes them to pop out -- sometimes when they are least expected.

Often when a man is confronted with something, he will react in the following order; first with his intellect (mind), because that is what he has grown to depend on, then he might act by doing something (body), then he may feel good or bad about what he has done (emotion).

A woman might react with her feelings first (emotion), then think about how she reacted (mind), then do something (body).

Anyone, male or female can act in any combination of ways, but more often than not they lead with their strongest most habitual response at the expense of the other two.

What would it be like if someone reacted with all three simultaneously, in a balanced way?

This is one of the goals of integrating the shadow in the process of individuation, and subsequently one of the rewards of personal power a shaman gets from getting swallowed by the jaguar.

These three primary inner energies have been characterized throughout myth and history in many ways. The thinking mind is referred to as knowledge and wisdom, the moving body is referred to as energy and power, while the feeling of emotion is referred to as love. On one end of the spectrum, the modern divide and conquer scientific mind set has given mind the most attention. Energetically it is the most stable. On the other end, emotion is the quickest, most mercurial, and hardest to control. The body usually serves the other two, though it holds deep wisdom of its own that is often ignored.

The Inca view of reality is a shamanic one that has three worlds; the upper world, represented by the condor, which has a rose color and is thought of as love (emotion). The middle world is represented by the jaguar or puma, and has an electric blue color signifying power (body). The lower world is represented by the serpent which has a gold color, signifying wisdom (mind). When the three are combined in harmony and unity, together they create a beautiful electric violet hue.

It is interesting to note the ways these three energies have been depicted in stories, particularly when we take into account how secondary characters mirror the inner life of the protagonist. The most striking example of this is in **The Wizard of Oz** where we have Dorothy on her hero's quest to find her way home. Her three primary allies are the tin man, who wants a heart (love -emotion), the cowardly lion, who wants courage (power - body), and the scarecrow, who wants a brain (wisdom - mind).

Aside from plotting a grand adventure with fascinating characters this philosophy has practical applications for writers as a whole as it holds the key to overcoming writer's block.

When a writer finds themselves "blocked" in their writing they are energetically stuck between their intellect and their emotions. Initially the words don't come, then they get emotional and worried when they won't, which makes the situation worse. The secret to freeing yourself from the energetic trap between your mind and your emotion is to move the trapped energy into your moving body to balance things out and give it some place to go. This means that instead of trying to force things, get up and take a walk, work in the garden, go to the gym, or do some other relatively mindless physical action and forget about your story or project.

A shaman's path is one of mastering energy. If you take a break like this, by moving the energy you master it, free yourself and give your subconscious time to process the problem at hand. When you return to the project, *the solution to your "block" will come*. By understanding and following the principles demonstrated here, the answers will always come from your trusty subconscious.

The Spine of the Journey

T he beginning of the Hero's Journey starts with an inciting incident that upsets the balance of the protagonist's life and ignites their quest to restore the balance.

In this diagram from *Story*, Robert McKee shows how the Quest describes the flow of conflict in a story. The + and - (the two circles) represent the positive and negative tug-of-war of conflict in the backstory before the inciting incident. The 'Spine' represents the through-line/timeline in the story. The conscious and unconscious desires describe the drive behind the external and internal journeys.

From *Robert McKee's "Story"*

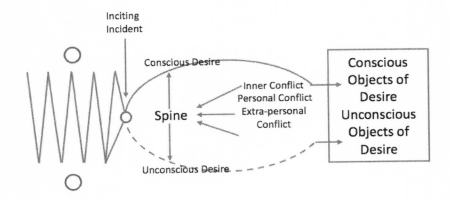

The inner, personal, and extra-personal conflicts represent the types of pressure that bear on the protagonist as the story progresses and the conscious and unconscious objects of desire represent the journeys' goals.

This dynamic can be played out on many levels with layers of complexity. Not only can subplots of secondary characters contain this element to varying degrees, but dual protagonists can mirror each other and change roles, alternating their position back and forth along the progression of the story's spine as a result of their own transformations on the journey.

This is what happens in the popular film ***Thelma & Louise***. In the beginning of the film, Louise is the stronger, more organized of the two, and the leader. Thelma is ditzy, scattered, and unfocused as well as being dependent on Louise. Exactly mid-point in the film, they reverse roles. Thelma becomes the leader and Louise becomes the dependent one. Their conscious desire arcing along the top of the spine is freedom and their unconscious desire arcing along the bottom of the spine is death, which mirrors their desire for freedom as it can be seen as the ultimate freedom.

The film ends with their car going off a cliff in mid-air. The audience knows it is going to a fiery finish, but that is not shown. Mid-air makes for a better finish by leaving the audience room to ponder. As a secondary point of interest, the inciting incident in this film does not occur until about twenty minutes into it.

Another great example of dual protagonists who mirror each other and change roles on their journey through the spine of the story is ***Terminator 2: Judgment Day***. In the beginning of the film, Sarah Connor is struggling to save mankind along with her son John while The Terminator is seen as a heartless, soulless killing machine. As the film progresses Sarah becomes the heartless, soulless killing machine and The Terminator becomes increasingly human by becoming a father figure to John, (With a sense of humor.), and by ultimately becoming Christ-like and selfless by sacrificing himself for the greater good of humanity.

Another way of visualizing the spine of the story as it unfolds along its path is the basic three-act structure that includes character set-up, an inciting incident, and conflict development that builds to a climax, ending in a resolution.

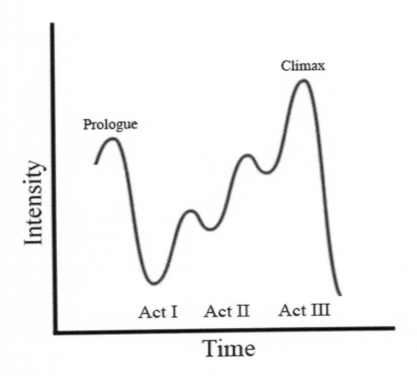

The number of events over time are represented by frequency and the height of the waveform represents the amount of energy it has, labeled here as Intensity. As the writer creator, you have the ability to shorten or lengthen the duration of any or all of these events. The first peak of Act One on this wave represents a climax. The resolution of this climax drains the tension from it, but it also creates a new problem, which rises with the next peak of Act Two. This resolution in turn sends us into Act Three for the biggest climax which brings things to an end in what is called a *denouement.*

The "moving crucible" of the protagonist is shamanic transformation in the story moment as it moves along the path of the spine like the fiery spark that travels along a fuse to ignite the explosion that is the climax.

Point of View

Point of View, otherwise known as POV has nuances that come into play when deciding who the protagonist of the story is as well as who it is that is narrating the story.

Shamans navigate multiple realities because they realize that their power lies in how they filter, see, and react to the realms that they come in contact with by manipulating their perception with the knowledge that all they experience ultimately comes through what is known as radical subjectivity.

Most newer writers choose first person, as it feels the most natural, but in dramatic works it has complexities and limitations that writers need to be aware of.

Three primary points of view are used in fiction writing and each has its own conventions for usage.

First person is the world seen directly through the eyes of the protagonist and is told in his or her voice. You can only stay in this one view point. You cannot write "meanwhile back at the ranch" in someone else's perspective. You cannot move about freely in time space and location - unless the protagonist narrates a flashback.

Having said that, a masterpiece of first person narrative that seems to break all the rules but does not is ***All the King's Men***, by Robert Penn Warren. It is well worth the read if you are looking to understand all the possibilities of a first person viewpoint.

Mysteries, especially the hard-boiled detective types, are written in first person so the reader gets the information at the same time the protagonist does and attempts to solve the puzzle of the crime along with them. In this case the limitation of the viewpoint works to the advantage of the storyteller. In first person you have only one place where the camera's viewpoint is located - through the eyes of the protagonist. This is the selective filter that the world you are exploring is seen through. The only exception that might change the "camera placement" is if the protagonist is narrating a scene that is different from the actual time of the "story moment". Warren does this quite effectively in **All the King's Men**.

Second person POV is not used much and can be tricky, but applied creatively it can be produce great results. It is usually more effective in short fiction. Not many novels are written in this POV, but it can be done. **Bright Lights, Big City** by Jay McInerney is a good example of this POV being used successfully.

Third person is the most commonly used POV and it is usually used in past tense, primarily because it has the most flexibility. Many beginning writers write in present tense because they are trying to bring more immediacy to their story, but this is difficult to do and it often draws attention to the writing. If you have a solid grasp of third person past tense, you can bring more than enough immediacy to your work. This is not to say that longer works of fiction cannot be written in present tense. It has been done, and remember there are no rules, but any time the writing draws attention to itself, you run the risk of distracting your readers from the fictional dream that you have worked so hard to create. Present tense can be more effective in short fiction to get a particular feeling or sensibility, but it is mostly used in screenplays where its use is a necessity.

In third person you can move around in time, space, location and viewpoint for more varied perspectives. You can use third person omniscient for a broader more wide ranging outlook and you can move in "up close and personal" in what's called third person close where you can show inner thoughts mixed with dialogue and perception. When you do this, inner thoughts should be treated as dialogue as it *is* dialogue between the character and themselves, only you don't need quotation marks for what is internal. You can have a lot of fun playing with levels of conflict having characters saying one thing, thinking another, and maybe even doing something totally different.

You can also have a narrator who is not the protagonist telling the story using a convention that can be called "Grandma on her rocking chair on the front porch", or "Kruk in front of the fire telling about the hunt". A great example of this is Chief Broom in Ken Kesey's **One Flew Over the Cucko's Nest**. Most people think it is McMurphy's story. Though it is about McMurphy, Chief Broom is the narrator and it is actually Chief Broom's story.

You can use multiple points of view in third person. As a general rule, the more points of view you show, the longer the work should be, but the more you stay in one point of view, the more your audience will care about and identify with your character. Though you will see it done in published works, jumping around from head to head within a scene dilutes the POV and creates a greater distance between your readers and the characters, making readers care less about them, and it is totally unnecessary.

Watch supporting characters in movies. We know what they are thinking by what they say and what they do. You can also study books on body language to learn how people show what they are thinking and feeling, then watch to see how actors do this in films. In fiction this can be done without jumping around from head to head. In my novel **Land Without Evil** the story is told in a broad scope in third person, but there is only one viewpoint character who is the microcosm for the bigger conflict that is going on around him.

If you do tell a story through multiple viewpoints it is best to give definitive indicators that you are changing POV. Changing at chapter breaks are best, but if you do change mid-chapter, a space break is in order to signal your audience that they will be seeing things through a different set of eyes. In film this is easy to do with scene breaks and editing cuts.

While in a unique POV use all of the senses. The more visceral, physical sensations you have, the tighter the POV. When a reader feels these sensations, it strikes a universal chord in them, because they can relate to the sensation/feeling which causes them to identify with it.

If you think of your viewpoint character as the lens of the camera where we experience subjectivity, or as stated earlier, an expression of the whole, interpreted through a different vibratory lens, then the focus as to how far internal or external we are can be gauged, whether depicting inner thought, dialogue, or action in past, present, or future. By adjusting this "camera focus" you can create engaging characters that your readers identify with and care about; *because they identify with them.*

Using the camera analogy, consider it when you are starting paragraphs and scenes. Each paragraph can be seen as a subtle camera, (perspective) shift. Dialogue exchanges are a good example of this. Like a good director, pay attention to where the camera is.

Every time you have a new scene, you need to set the scene and give stage direction so the characters are doing something in a setting, otherwise you have "talking heads, making it a struggle for readers to *visualize* what is happening. Keep the setting and action alive and flowing with judicious placement of significant details that draw a distinctive environment.

Character Development

J ust as we in the "real world" are driven by hopes, desires, lust, fear, love, greed, hunger, and all the rest, so it is with the characters we create. What makes them do what they do and say what they say? What inspires them? Your characters are vehicles for the motivations that you give them.

You need to clothe these vehicles in distinctive and memorable ways. How do they look, think, act, and talk? What mannerisms do they have? Habits? Fetishes? Are they missing one arm, or are they picture - perfect handsome or beautiful? What makes them stand out from the crowd? How will your readers remember them? When they do come on the scene, there should be no question of seeing them clearly and knowing without question who they are.

If you've ever watched a play, you'll notice that each character makes an "entrance". So it should be with your fiction. This is the first time the reader is introduced to the character, and first impressions *do* count. The more important a character is, the more attention to detail they deserve.

Sometimes an entrance is preceded by talk and descriptions from characters already on stage, increasing anticipation while giving the entrance character even more import.

Regardless of whether your entering character has been "announced" or not, this entrance scene has to give the initial descriptions of him or her in more detail and it has to be done without stalling the forward momentum of the story. The best way to do this is to combine description with action, so there is always movement in a manner that slips the descriptions to the reader as the action moves along without them having to stop and think about it. Here is an example from Stephen King's **Duma Key**.

I had pictured a bald, skinny, professorial man with blazing brown eyes -- an Italian Ben Kingsley -- but Dario Nunnuzi turned out to be fortyish, plump, courtly, and possessed a full head of hair. I was close on the eyes, though. They didn't miss a trick. I saw them widen once -- slightly but perceptibly -- when Wireman carefully unwrapped the painting I'd brought, Roses Grow from Shells.

This approach prevents a static, lifeless, adjective infested description and ensures a living, active, dynamic story, plot, and character movement that rockets forward, revealing the character as it goes, while fueling increased momentum for the narrative. When you do describe a character or any other description like a setting, it is best to do it in a "series of threes", in the same form as the cliché, "tall, dark, and handsome".

Get the initial description down first by drawing a well-defined picture that is dynamic, not static. Don't get caught in the trap of thinking that you have to get all this detail and back story in up front and be done with it so you don't have to worry about it any more.

One of the basic tenets of shamanism is transformation, which in fiction means that your characters should change from the beginning of the story to the end. Use significant details, purposely leaving out key points that raise questions in your reader's mind, enticing them to keep turning the pages to find the answers to the mystery. Dole out important details as clues and puzzle pieces. Create intrigue.

Keeping all this in mind, your characters should be introduced in the beginning, and as the story unfolds, so should your characters. The term "character development" did not come to be for no reason. Your characters should develop the same way photographic film develops. When you first put the photographic paper in the developer you see the beginnings of blurry images. As the process continues, they become sharper and you begin to see details that you didn't see at first. As they accumulate, and your story and your characters develop, your story takes form.

One of the most important things to give each character is one or more distinctive "character tags" that are flags to let the reader know who they're dealing with. They can be physical, like a missing eye, hair color, complexion, stature and build, or they can be the way they talk, mannerisms, how they smell, how they walk, or how they dress. The possibilities are endless.

I heard the door to the study open and the subtle fragrance of Tatiana drifted to me on the breeze. I knew without having to turn around that it was Priscilla.

Maybe their personal hygiene is lacking so they smell like something that just crawled out of a cesspool. Use your character tags as reminders as you move through the story, so the reader's right there with you, thinking that's Hannibal all right; Chianti, fava beans, and liver.

It's not difficult to come up with thumbnail sketches of central characters. The hard part comes when you flesh them out and make them unique creatures whose triumphs, tribulations, and transformation will be worth a reader's time to share. Give them emotions and feelings that are universal, something your readers can hook into and *identify* with. If you can get your reader to identify and react emotionally, they will have empathy for your creations and will care about what happens to them, good or bad. This is what it means to hook your readers.

Get to know your characters *yourself*, as well as you can. During the course of your project you will be living with them every moment, both sleeping and waking. Prepare yourself, because you *will* miss them when you come to the end of a long project. It's the writer's version of post-partum blues.

Every writer has their own way of becoming intimate with their characters. Some work at a deeper, intuitive level, others prefer a more structured approach. There are a number of ways to accomplish this, one of the more popular being the use of what is known as a "Character Dossier".

By taking the time to create a dossier, or some other type of vivid character sketch, the focus you put on it will help bring that character into focus *for you*. The more you know about your characters, the more "real" they become to you. Anything that helps the process of bringing them to life in the mind of their author is valuable. If your characters don't live for you, how can they live for anybody else?

Many writers don't need to work their characters out on paper. They already know them intimately and base their makeup on people they've known and observed. Don't be afraid to use movie stars or public figures as models for your descriptions, only don't mention their names. Simply describe their appearance and mannerisms. Like the shaman who manipulates his own radical subjectivity, every reader brings their own perceptions and experiences to a story when they read, so each will envision your characters in their own unique way.

What motivated that nice, gentle, quiet young man to lure teenage boys and young men upstairs to his apartment where he butchered them, ate them, and kept the leftovers in his refrigerator? What motivated one man to send thousands to their deaths in gas chambers and another to give his own life so others could live? These are your characters' reason for being that bring life to your fiction. These are the things that bring life to your characters and what makes them tick.

Relationships

In shamanism everything is connected to everything else. Plants, animals, man, and elemental spirits all interact and affect each other in visible and invisible ways. In fiction, regardless of the time, place, setting, or the players that are woven into your story, it is all about relationships. The way your characters interact, connect, and collide should be emotionally felt by them. If their emotional lives ring true, your readers will become involved in the story, because they will feel the same things your characters feel.

When you set out to tell the story, one of your first decisions will be to choose whose point of view you want to tell your story through. Whose eyes, ears and emotions will we be seeing the story filtered through? Better still, whose eyes will give your story the greatest emotional and dramatic impact? This viewpoint character will color the way the whole story plays out for your readers.

Fewer points of view make it easier for your readers to identify and care about fewer characters and it gives them better focus. The more point of view characters you bring to the party, the harder you have to work to make your readers care about them.

There is much that can be done to flesh out characters by seeing them through each other's eyes. How does one person's speech and actions influence another's emotional viewpoint? How do two characters talking about a third make the viewpoint character think and feel?

Imagine a child in a police station watching and listening to his father talk to a burly detective about his missing mother. Through the dialogue we can give the mother's description, habits, fears and routines. We add another dimension by showing how the kid feels. Through the kid's eyes we can give descriptions of the two men, how they talk and look. How do *they* make him feel?

Is his father nervous, or does he come across as uncaring? Is he leaving out important information that the kid knows he's lying about? How about the cop? How is he reacting to what the father says? What kind of questions is he asking? How does he look at the kid?

Are you getting to know these on-stage characters a little? How about the off-stage one? You're definitely getting to know the kid. Do you see how much work this scene does? There's talking and thinking and action, all going on simultaneously; the plot is being advanced, character is being revealed, and your story is alive.

The ups and downs, the good, the bad, and the ugly between people are what makes a story, whether it be two warring clans, countries, or individuals. Even if it is a man against a machine, technology, a country, or nature; no matter what the scenario, the story is about relationships. This is what makes stories accessible to readers, because when everything is said and done, the story is about people and we as people care what happens to other people. It's part of being human and a cornerstone of good fiction.

The urges and desires that stem from the motivations talked about earlier propel your creations toward each of their destinies, sometimes together, sometimes at odds with one another, sometimes both. This is how it is in real life and this is how it is in fiction.

The emotional ties your characters have to their hopes, dreams, fears, desires, possessions, and to each other are the ties that bind them in your fictional world. The emotional investment your creations have in these things will touch your readers at a deeper level, giving them an emotional investment in what happens to your characters. It is also what will keep your readers turning the pages.

PHANTASTIC FICTION

A Jaded Outlook

Every scene should reinforce character through the mood that it sets in the same way that a shaman sees the world through the lens of radical subjectivity. Using the little boy in the police station as a model, the details of your setting should be filtered through your viewpoint character's eyes and their perspective should reflect their moods and feelings by the way *they* see the world. The whole description should be influenced by how they see things and it should contain metaphors that reinforce their thoughts and impressions. The weather, the way they see the color of a room, how they see a building, a car, animals, people, and the actions of others should all reflect their mood.

Instead of overusing flowery adjectives in an attempt to barrage readers with details that you hope will make the setting come to life, choose each word with care and use active verbs instead of adjectives whenever possible. Adjectives are static and paint a still picture. Active verbs are just that: *active*, as your scene should be. Combine your character's actions with their setting. What they do is as important as where they do it. Energy should be inherent in every word, phrase, and paragraph. The setting itself should be a character or better still a reflection of your viewpoint character. Make the scene carry its weight and more.

In **The Great Gatsby**, Fitzgerald gives us our first impressions of the wild, frivolous party atmosphere and flighty attitudes of the wealthy through the eyes of the naive Nick Caraway who lived in the less fashionable, West Egg.

77

... A breeze blew through the room, blew curtains in one end and out the other like pale flags, twisting them up toward the frosted wedding cake ceiling, and then rippled over the wine-colored rug, making a shadow on it as the wind does on the sea.

Look at the active verbs. This world is alive with a breeze that is twisting and rippling. Other details that paint the picture are a frosted wedding cake ceiling and a wine colored rug. One sentence here certainly does a lot of work. Now look how the mood builds and suddenly changes by the action of one character.

The only stationary object in the room was an enormous couch on which two young women were buoyed up as though upon an anchored balloon. They were both in white, and their dresses were rippling and fluttering as if they had just been blown back in after a short flight around the house. I must have stood for a few moments listening to the whip and snap of the curtains and the groan of a picture on the wall. Then there was a boom as Tom Buchanan shut the rear windows and the caught wind died out about the room, and the curtains and the rugs and the two young women ballooned slowly to the floor.

Is Tom a party pooper or what? Do his actions make you uneasy? Maybe hint at something more sinister? The setting here shows us these characters, their moods and their actions through Nick's viewpoint. If he were angry or depressed we probably wouldn't see a wedding cake ceiling and a wine colored rug. Instead we might see a rancid, cottage cheese ceiling and a blood colored rug.

Don't forget to use *all* the senses. In this initial description you can almost taste the wine and wedding cake.

In another example from Stephen King's **The Shining**, the viewpoint character is Jack Torrance, a smart-ass loser with a drinking problem who resents authority. Observe how Jack sees the world. This scene starts with Ullman, the man who interviews and hires Jack. Ullman is the one scrawling the note.

He scrawled a note on a pad he took from his inner coat pocket (each sheet bore the legend *From the Desk of Stuart Ullman* in bold black script), tore it off, and dropped it into the out basket. It sat there looking lonesome. The pad disappeared back into Ullman's jacket pocket like the conclusion of a magician's trick. Now you see it, Jacky-boy, now you don't. This guy is a real heavyweight.

They had resumed their original positions, Ullman behind the desk and Jack in front of it, interviewer and interviewee, supplicant and reluctant patron. Ullman folded his neat little hands on the desk blotter and looked directly at Jack, a small, balding man in a banker's suit and a quiet gray tie. The flower in his lapel was balanced off by a small lapel pin on the other side. It read simply STAFF in small gold letters.

In this passage we're close inside Jack's thoughts. From the way he sees things, we learn as much if not more about Jack than we do about Ullman.

In the real world (so to speak), the way a person lives and the way they decorate their house and their surroundings are an extension of themselves. There is the little old lady with fragile, dainty white doilies, flowered curtains, and pictures of the grandchildren covering the walls, or the high-powered businessman with his spacious mahogany desk, silver pen and pencil set and wall of leather bound volumes. How about an Asian family with an altar to their ancestors in their living room and the exotic and sometimes not so exotic smells that go with their diet, or the Jewish family with the symbols and customs of their religion. Granted these are clichéd examples, but they make the point.

Like the shaman, the reality you create is filtered through the different vibratory lens of your viewpoint character's perceptions. Show how they see the world and the people in it. Show your reader their world by what they surround themselves with. Use your settings as a tool to describe characters so that the passage not only sets scene, but also defines character and moves the story. Say more with less. The more you make each word carry its weight and perform more than one function, the more life and dynamics your story will have.

Pacing

The pacing and structure of a work of fiction are critical for its success. A shaman masters their reality by mastering the energies of it, which is what the writer/creator must do to create a living, vibrant world.

Aside from the obvious overt tension of the scene itself, the reader's subconscious must be tugged at in as many ways as possible. Good dramatic writing has hidden, underlying levels of tension that pulls unseen rubber bands to propel the narrative forward. The careful choice of punctuation, tone, word choice, phrases, and sentence structure can be combined to produce varying levels of tension.

Punctuation gives the reader breathing spaces which can be used to create hidden tension for the reader. Commas are momentary stops, periods are harder ones; semicolons fall somewhere in between. If it's a mellow and relaxed descriptive scene where your characters are at peace, long, languishing sentences can lull the reader into a relaxing mood. Here is an example:

Shimmering fingers of gold bathed the valley in a warm embrace and the smells of jasmine and honeysuckle drifted to her on the gentle breeze as the sun sank behind the emerald hills of Deer Valley.

Notice the way the longer sentence adds layers of relaxing details, using soft, caressing active verbs -- shimmering fingers that bathed and embraced. Not only does the valley look relaxing, it *feels* relaxing.

Here's another example using short, hard sentences.

The viper sank its fangs into his eye. He screamed and the pain lanced him. Hot. Blinding. Agonizing.

The short hard stops create a halting, breathless feeling. Something like the way it would feel when a viper sank its fangs into your eye -- the way the thoughts and sensations would hit the victim's brain. Stabbing. Lancing. Definitely not as comforting as being bathed and embraced.

Now we'll combine the long run-on sentence with a series of comma pauses to create a feeling of rushing and falling headlong out of control.

Chris slid down the side of the hill, tumbling, falling, spinning, his world a jumbled blur of whipping branches, rocks, and crumbling dirt.

Can you feel the way the words and the action tumbled along on the force of their own momentum.

One more. A series of sentence fragments to portray a disjointed mental state.

My God, she stabbed him -- blood -- splattering -- his shoes - he gasped as his finger fell to the floor. A flash of steel - another finger - now his wrist -- blood jetting from the stump...

Get the picture? Right hook. Left jab. Keep 'em reeling.

Tone and word choice are as important as sentence length and structure. Active verbs are always best. Notice in the stabbing sentence that the blood splatters and jets, the knife flashes. In the Deer Valley scene the sun bathes and embraces. In each of these sentences the tone is obvious. The mood and mental state of the viewpoint character color the perceptions and should be reflected in the choice of words and punctuation that convey the feelings and mood. To a military commander, telephone poles lining the side of the road might look like sentinels standing guard. To a six year old kid, they might look like Lincoln Logs.

A good example of this can be found in **The Shining**. When Jack the writer goes to the library in the fall just before being barricaded into the Overlook Hotel for the winter, the withered flowers lining the front walk of the library are described as "the corpses of the flowers". What kind of image and foreshadowing does the word "corpse" invoke? He could have simply said withered flowers.

If someone's upset, a fiery red sunset might look like a blistering, puss-filled boil on the verge of exploding. If they're happy and content it might be a rose-colored sunset. Don't hesitate to use setting details to reinforce your viewpoint character's moods, but don't overdo it. Notice how you perceive your world when you're in different moods.

Effective dramatic writing should be loaded with layers and levels of emotions and images that support and underscore the narrative while bringing the fictional world to life for your characters *and* your readers. Loaded imagery and structure will strike your reader's conscious and subconscious awareness, bringing more depth and feeling to their experience. With these techniques in mind, analyze some of your favorite writers and find out why and how their writing affected you, then incorporate what works into your own writing.

Creating Suspense

S uspense can be defined as the state or quality of being undecided, uncertain, or doubtful, a state which shamans know well. It is an integral part of their world. The word suspense comes from the word suspend which means to hang so as to allow free movement or to keep in abeyance. So how do you keep your readers hanging (as in the edge of their chair) and in abeyance?

By holding back pieces of the puzzle -- just the right pieces revealed at the proper time, then giving the reader inside information that the characters are unaware of.

Alfred Hitchcock, one of the all time brilliant masters of suspense gave this definition of the difference between "suspense" and "surprise" in an interview with French film director Francois Truffaut.

"There is a distinct difference between 'suspense' and 'surprise', and yet many pictures continually confuse the two. I'll explain what I mean.

We are now having a very innocent little chat. Let us suppose that there is a bomb underneath this table between us. Nothing happens, and then all of a sudden, 'Boom!' There is an explosion. The public is surprised, but prior to this surprise, it has seen an absolutely ordinary scene, of no special consequence. Now, let us take a suspense situation. The bomb is underneath the table and the public knows it, probably because they have seen the anarchist place it there. The public is aware that the bomb is going to explode at one o'clock and there is a clock in the decor. The public can see that it is a quarter to one. In these conditions this same innocuous conversation becomes fascinating because the public is participating in the scene. The audience is longing to warn the characters on the screen: 'You shouldn't be talking about such trivial matters. There's a bomb beneath you and it's about to explode!'

In the first case we have given the public fifteen seconds of surprise at the moment of the explosion. In the second we have provided them with fifteen minutes of suspense. The conclusion is that whenever possible the public must be informed. Except when the surprise is a twist, that is, when the unexpected ending is, in itself, the highlight of the story."

In the opening scenes of a story, create as many unanswered questions as you can. By leaving out selected details, questions will be raised in your reader's mind that he or she will read on to find the answers to. By putting in hints that foreshadow upcoming events, more questions are raised that will pull your reader deeper into the unfolding drama.

By using misdirection, distractions, and false clues known as red herrings when putting in planted information, you can distract your reader, then when the penny finally drops, he or she will be pleasantly surprised. Whenever this happens to you reading someone else's work, go back and examine how they pulled it off. Study how filmmakers do it and apply their techniques to your own writing.

The pacing of your narrative and the timing of when certain information is imparted should be orchestrated for maximum dramatic effect. If you give information to your reader that the character doesn't know about, you can play cat and mouse with your readers and characters, slowly building toward an inevitable climax.

The tauter you pull the rubber band of suspense, the closer you can drag your reader to the edge of the seat, hopefully right to the edge.

For a good lesson in suspense, close your eyes the next time you take a shower and spend some time thinking about Norman Bates.

Significant Details

Shamans are masters of perception and learn very quickly that they have to pay attention to every detail and every nuance of their world, whether it be the sight of a coyote or a crow, the song of a bird, or a shift in the wind. To them everything in interconnected nature has a message and some of the messages have greater import than others. They must learn to pay attention to everything, especially those details that carry the most significance.

As the human race evolves, so does its language and technology, which continually brings us new ways of seeing and envisioning the world with new ways of thinking and communicating. With the advent of film and television, what used to be told in words and static pictures, can now be seen in a myriad of images from all over the world and beyond at the mere flick of a finger. High-quality phone, video, and internet capabilities allow us to transport thoughts and images from anywhere in the world, to anywhere in the world in seconds.

This phenomena has a dramatic impact on the way our minds form concepts and structure thought. Like the shaman in nature, the world is literally at our fingertips. Because we have such ready, accessible input to our sensory receptors, it has become simpler to evoke images in our minds with words. How broad or how detailed do the strokes need to be to paint moving, living, vivid images on the screens and canvases of the minds of readers?

The right strokes, deftly executed, define the meaning of "significant details". Which details are important? Which are not?

When do we show specific detail and when do we hold back? What should we show and what do we discard?

The details that we choose are tied to the pace and setting of the story. If there's a fast action scene where someone is getting hit in the face by a man with a big ring on his hand, you wouldn't describe the ring in all its intricate detail, because the viewpoint character is going to be seeing it in fast motion. No more than a flash of gold, if that. Depending on the viewpoint and the speed of the punch, the whole hand might be nothing more than a blur.

If the ring stamps an imprint on someone's forehead, and they're studying it in the mirror, then we're in a slower, literally, self-examining moment and have the time and the pace to show more detail. Is it significant? Is the imprint on your character's forehead the Nazi death sign that has been found on the heads of four dead people?

When a character, scene, setting, or action are first introduced, that is the time to describe them fully. ***Land Without Evil*** centers around an ecstatic dance that has elaborated details of dress, feathers, ritual, rattles, and other implements. The first time this dance is described, it is done so with fully fleshed out descriptions. Every time it occurs later in the book, a handful of carefully selected significant details are used to give the framework for the event and the reader's mind fills in the rest.

The same is true for character descriptions. A detailed description is given when a character makes their entrance and select character tags are given in subsequent encounters. A good way to think of these carefully chosen character tags and significant details is the idea of a visual refresh.

In old television tube technology an electron beam strikes the phosphor coating on the inside of the tube's viewing surface, causing it to light up and glow. Before its luminescence fades a scanning beam hits the phosphor again, relighting it at a refresh rate that is fast enough to eliminate any flicker that might be visible to the naked eye. This analogy applies to the use of significant details in keeping your fictional reality vibrant and alive in the mind's eye of your readers.

Whenever something new and unique is brought in to your created universe, particularly in works of science fiction or historical works that have items unique to those worlds, be sure to define them in context, the first time you use them. If you use a few of these terms judiciously in description and dialogue, you can create the illusion of being in a different time and place and you can create the illusion of characters speaking in a different language.

Land Without Evil is set in the jungle of ancient Paraguay and the Indians in the story are speaking Guarani. In the passage that follows, two terms used to describe concepts that a modern reader would not know are introduced.

Tekó achy are the base passions and evil appetites of humans, imperfections thought of as the animal soul.

Ywy mará ey is the Guarani name for the Land Without Evil.

"You do not have to fall to the crushing weight of *techó-achy*," he continued. **"You can free yourself from the weight of your faults, lighten your bodies, and reach perfection by abandoning the food and the ways of the whites. You must journey to where you can dance until your bodies rise above the earth and fly across the great primeval sea to the Land Without Evil."**

A murmur rose from the crowd.

"*Ywy Mará Ey*, a paradise of abundance and wealth. True immortality awaits you there. You do not have to die to enter. It is a real world that lies in the place where the sun rises. Only dancing believers dwell there. To find paradise you must..."

The writer brings passion and words to the story, the reader brings his or her own experiences and visualizations which make each reading experience as unique and varied as the people that pick up the book. The reader brings their own thoughts, concepts, fears, and prejudices; their own unique perspective of the world, which comes to bear on the words that they read, influencing how they experience the story. If the details are laid with deft strokes, your audience will see the world the same way your viewpoint characters do.

When your reader experiences the story along with your characters, they become actively involved in the story, living and experiencing it with the characters.

Reading is a shared act of creation between the writer and the reader. A dance of the minds. The writer leads with a firm hand and the reader follows, putting themselves into the hands of their guide as he or she pulls them along, stepping here, stepping there.

Choose your details carefully, picking the ones that bring maximum dramatic impact and the most powerful, active imagery, and you will flesh out a living, breathing reality in your reader's mind that will swallow them into a meaningful world that you have created out of your mind.

Suspension of Disbelief

The moment a reader picks up a work of fiction they have entered into an unspoken contract with the writer to co-create the world the writer is portraying. Implicit in this contract is the reader's willingness to "suspend his disbelief". It is up to the writer to keep his end of the contract and use his abilities to make this leap of faith painless and invisible. This is critical in writing fiction, and even more so in the genres of horror, fantasy, and science fiction. Not only must the writer create this alternate reality, but they must keep it believable and do it smooth and seamlessly without jarring the reader from the spell they're weaving.

Depending on the genre and the story, there are many different methods. If you've done your research you will have plenty to work with. It's well worth the time to study the genre you're writing for with an eye toward the conventions and techniques your favorite writers use. How did they get *you* to suspend *your* disbelief?

Just as in the radically subjective world view of a shaman, all writing no matter how bizarre the setting or characters is about relationships in an environment, whether it's between people and people, humans and Ewoks, Androids and humans, or androids and Robocops. It all comes down to relationships between two or more sentient beings. It is the writer's job to tap into *universal* thoughts and emotions. This is what makes fictional realities believable for readers.

No matter what the world or the circumstances, physical, tactile, sensual and emotional sensations are universal experiences that readers relate to and identify with. In horror it's the chill dancing down the spine, the dry throat, cold sweat, or shaking hands. These are things everyone has experienced. In science fiction, you might have an alien whose eyeball gets sexually stimulated every time it looks at a rhododendron. Can you imagine what that might feel like? If so, put it into words and make it come to life for your reader. In fantasy, it's often a sense of awe and wonder at beings with mythical powers. It can also be a sense of disorientation from being whisked away to another world, like middle earth or fairy land. What does it feel like to experience awe or disorientation? In romance it's the throes of passion. In mysteries and thrillers, more often than not, it's the instinct for self-preservation.

How skillful are you at world building to make someone suspend their disbelief?

If you're working in a more contemporary setting, along with the universal sensations and experiences of life, bring in the every day things readers can relate to, particularly brand names that define the world like Coca-Cola, Budweiser or Wonder Bread. Stores and places like Starbucks, Seven-Eleven, MacDonald's, or a funky little bar in Tijuana.

In a horror story, at what point do we cross over from "normal reality" into the world of the bizarre and horrific? Does it happen immediately or can you pin it down to one word, sentence, or moment in time when it starts getting weird? Pick up a copy of Stephen King's **Pet Sematary** and read the first few pages. It starts out normal. When and where does it slip into weirdness?

In science fiction and fantasy you can jump right into the alien world/reality, because your reader is more willing to give you this suspension of disbelief, but science fiction and fantasy fans are more discerning than average readers. They live for these strange details of alternate realities and alien points of view. These genres are more works of imagination than most others. It's more important to strive for originality, particularly in your choice of settings.

Make your readers live through your characters so they *become* your characters. In science fiction and fantasy worlds keep everything consistent using exotic descriptions for your characters and their environment as well as words and sensations, particularly when it comes to measurements, units of time and distance. You can't have an exotic alien cross a desert at a hundred miles an hour. Have your character make the trip in two solar cycles or four centons. The same goes for smells. You can't have an extraterrestrial fry someone's brains with their particle disruptor and have the smoldering corpse smell like roast beef. An alien has no conception of what roast beef smells like. Your alien or mythical creature might smell colors and taste sound.

Put yourself in the alien mind and look at things from an "alien" perspective. This is the same thing shamans do when they navigate different realities.

It is up to the writer to make the world that inhabits their mind as real for their audience as it is for them. Universal experiences and sensations help to accomplish this. It's easy to take for granted that whoever reads your story will have the same familiarity with all of its details as you do.

It's similar to taking a ride with someone to a destination that's familiar to you when you're supposed to give directions. You're so used to going there, you forget to tell them when to make a turn and before you know it you're off course. Be sure to provide plenty of significant details so they are sufficiently oriented in your world without struggling to find their way through it.

Foreshadowing and Misdirection

Since writing is a shared act of creation between the writer and their audience, the fictional world that comes into existence as a result of this union unfolds within a pace and dimension set forth by the author in the same way a shaman structures their view of the reality they are navigating. Like a dance between two partners, the book is presented to the reader like an invitation to dance from the writer.

As the writer leads, they unfold the story through a series of accumulating details, each of which is a defining stroke in their creation. As fictional story time moves forward, the unfolding world becomes more defined with each successive stroke because of significant details strategically placed at key story points by the author.

These story points provide opportunities for foreshadowing and misdirection. If done right, the "Aha" moments in which your reader feels intellectually superior will occur as the result of the accumulation of details that have been laid down ahead of time by the calculating writer.

Foreshadowing provides the reader with highly significant details that can seem innocuous at first and if planted skillfully, are almost forgotten, until that final climactic "moment of truth" when the penny drops and the incongruities come together in a flash of insight where it all makes sense.

The payoff of this flash is a carefully planned event that built on what preceded it, detail by detail until the moment of detonation. The highly significant details that bring about the "Aha" moment should be sprinkled throughout the narrative from the earliest possible points in the story to give the reader the information without drawing attention to itself. The best way to do this is through misdirection.

There are as many ways to use misdirection to plant foreshadowing seeds as there are foreshadowing details. As a general guideline, the writer gives the information in a manner that calls attention to the detail, then brings in a more immediate situation that overshadows the moment. This is how the hook is set.

Mesmerized, John watched the movement of the dancer's hips swaying to the beat of the music. Her eyes locked with his, then she winked and her fingers slid down to the edge of her bikini bottom, slowly tugging at it until he saw the first lines of a tattoo that for a moment looked like the other half of the map.

A hand slid up his thigh. He turned to see big, brown, doe like eyes challenge him with a wanton look.

Does she or doesn't she? Only the writer knows for sure. The story could go on for hundreds of pages, then at a critical time, the issue of the bikini tattoo could become a major one.

Another method of misdirection that works in conjunction with the previously described technique is to plant details that muddy the waters and distract your readers with red herrings. Use both methods and mix up the insignificant red herrings with the highly significant details to keep your readers guessing.

It is fun to figure out where and when to plant the seeds of your foreshadowing and fun to decide where and when they will blossom into something that makes mysterious and puzzling details make sense. Use foreshadowing and misdirection creatively and make sure you do it in a way that plays fair with your readers.

Combining Action with Description

While your characters are revealing themselves through conflict, they are moving and acting through the world you have created. Instead of stopping the action to paint a picture, your characters should always be doing something. Start scenes in the middle of already moving action, or start from a dead stop and build to a peak. Keep it varied and unpredictable, yet give it a rhythm.

Whenever possible, lead your readers to what appears to be an inevitable conclusion, then frustrate their expectations with a twist that surprises them, yet makes sense when everything that leads up to it is taken into consideration. This is exactly what happens in a shamanic journey.

There are times when people do "stop and smell the roses" like sitting atop mountain peaks, or looking out over sunsets, but there are also times when your creations gallop through barren, blistering, cactus-studded deserts; or stroll down dusty, unpaved, Tijuana side streets through mazes of battered taco carts.

Once your characters make their entrances, keep them moving. It doesn't always have to be big action. It can be something as intense and subtle as a prison yard stare from an angry biker or words muttered under someone's breath. A twitching finger or eyelid can at times be far more effective than an overt act of violence. Combine some of these small actions with a tight, confined setting and you have the proverbial "tempest in a teapot".

Two characters sitting together in an office can kill a story, but if you have one twiddling a pen, his imposing bulk behind a huge bulwark of a mahogany desk, staring down at a slight man in an ill-fitting suit trembling in a small, plastic chair, eyes looking everywhere but at his tormentor, your scene can have real pathos. How about a shy, lovesick, pimple-faced teenager sitting by himself in the corner of a restaurant watching a pretty waitress flitting from table to table with the beauty and grace of a butterfly?

If it's a reflective, meditative moment, their inner thoughts should be buzzing. What your people think and how they think can characterize and describe them as much, if not more than physical details. The settings they inhabit can enhance the impact of these moods and thoughts, sometimes provoking and stimulating them.

No matter what the circumstances, have your characters *doing* something. Don't be afraid to add significant details of their descriptions to their actions -- greasy hair, stubby hands, spindly legs, etc. Work toward making their actions and descriptions one and the same so your readers can not tell the difference. Done with finesse, you can slip them the descriptive details while they're not looking while adding texture and dimension to your narrative. The important thing is to keep it alive.

Every time a new scene is created the reader needs to be oriented in time and space as well as who they are in the scene with, fleshed out with settings, character descriptions, and action, combining action (stage direction), and descriptions. There should be a balance between action, description, inner thoughts, and dialogue. When there is too much information and back story given in inner thought and narrative, it can drift into "telling" instead of "showing". Although there are times when you want to tell things in narrative to keep the story moving, it is often better to give information in dialogue and acted out in scenes.

Dialogue

A great way to define a character is through dialogue as people reveal who they are by what they say and how they say it, but if you say things too directly simply to give information, you will be guilty of dialogue that is what screenwriters call "on the nose". Dialogue should create the illusion of speech. If you record an actual conversation and write it down, it does not come across as coherent, it will come across as disconnected non-sequiturs.

Many non-verbal details that do not come across in dialogue come into play when two people are communicating, including facial expressions, body language, gestures, and other nuances. There are also the inner thoughts of your characters which is a conversation with themselves. These should be treated the same as spoken dialogue in terms of pacing and the stimulus and response of spoken exchanges, without the quotation marks. Multiple layers of conflict can be explored bringing depth and complexity to your characters and your story when their thoughts, spoken words and actions are not in alignment.

Many beginning writers get caught up in attribution and go to great lengths to avoid what they see as a redundancy in using the word "said", replacing it with replied, interjected, responded, queried, etc., producing stilted, clunky exchanges along the lines of an amusing book on dialogue by William Noble titled ***Shut up! He Explained.***

In reality, the word "said" in dialogue exchanges is almost invisible to readers unless it is overused. Having characters doing something can replace the need for attribution and add impact to what they are saying and can even act as non-verbal punctuation.

John slammed his fist into the table. "I've had enough of your shit!"

As far as dialogue goes, when using a character's name, use it in context, by who is talking to them. If Captain John Smith is being addressed by another member of the military, he will be addressed and referred to as Captain Smith, but if his wife or close friend is talking to him, they will call him John.

The tone and content of the dialogue can also define who is saying it without attribution or action, especially in short rapid exchanges.

"What did you do it for?"

"I have no idea what you are talking about."

"Don't play stupid with me. We found the murder weapon in your trunk."

"I want to talk to my lawyer."

You can also create the illusion of a different spoken language by changing the order of the words in sentences and expressions. In English we say "big woman". In Spanish they reverse it and say "*mujer grande*" -- woman big.

Here is an example of what George Lucas did with Yoda, who embodies the essence of a shaman.

"When nine hundred years old you reach, look as good you will not." -- From ***Return of the Jedi***

Along these lines, accents and dialect should be implied with a few choice expressions that give a sense of the vernacular without going overboard.

"Y'all comin' home?"

Too much of this can make a reader work too hard and runs the risk of having the words call attention to themselves which can negatively impact the suspension of disbelief, but used judiciously, like spices in a good recipe, this kind of detail can bring authenticity to the fictional dream.

Characters should be doing things instead of having to say "said" all the time. It inserts action, helps to develop their character and description, and breaks up long strings of dialogue exchanges that could turn into "talking heads". Show more and tell less. If you say he frowned angrily, angrily is telling, frowned is showing. Show --

don't tell.

If you keep everything moving forward, your audience will never have the time to stop and ponder. Before they have the chance, the next action will be there to pull them further along to the next one. This is what makes a book a page turner that is hard to put down.

Showing and Telling

If you've spent any time in creative writing classes, writer's conferences, or writing workshops, then you've heard the admonition, show, *don't tell!* If you've never been in one of those situations, then this idea may be new to you. It's important to understand this concept if you want to write fiction that is living, active, and evocative.

Newer writers often slip into a mode where they *tell* you everything that happened instead of giving you the unfolding scene as a dramatic presentation that milks the action and dialogue for all that they are worth. Writers who do this are in a hurry to get all the back story details and information out of the way, so they can get on to the "good stuff". When done properly *everything they write should be "good stuff"*.

If the beginning is done right, presented dramatically with significant details added and some important details strategically left out, you will create a mystery that will make your readers want to find out more about what's missing.

Newer writers fall back into telling at different points throughout the story whenever they're in a hurry to impart information that they feel is necessary to the story, but not important enough to present dramatically. This makes the story read more like an outline than an engaging adventure. Often they do this because they don't know how to show passages of time, changes of place, and the long stretches of normal, mundane things that go on in people's lives, like paying bills, brushing their teeth, going to the dentist etc.

Fiction writers have to give the illusion of these things happening with minimal words, saving the full-on, fleshed out dramatic scenes for the moments that deserve to be exploited. If there is too much telling and not enough showing, then your fiction will follow the pattern described by a former paramedic, firefighter, state trooper when he described his job.

Long periods of monotonous boredom interspersed with short periods of intense, high-drama action.

For your story to be successful, you must connect all these dramatic scenes like a string of pearls with the so-called, non-dramatic parts interspersed with the pearls of drama in a way that keeps the heartbeat of your story pumping at a pace that you set. If done right, your structure will keep readers turning the pages without wearing them out from an overdose of tension, or putting them to sleep for lack of it.

Every scene needs action, but there are varying degrees of tension and conflict. What follows each scene depends on how high the tension is ratcheted in that scene.

Times of intense action need relief from their relentlessness with slower, introspective moments *that have to stay active*. In particularly intense moments, a dose of humor can be effective in bringing the much needed drop in pressure that gives your reader a chance to breathe. This is the definition of comic relief. If done with the right timing, it can be a masterful stroke, much appreciated by your audience.

Steven Spielberg's Oscar winning film ***Schindler's List*** has one of the most riveting moments of comic relief ever done. In this stark black and white scene rows of emaciated Jewish prisoners are lined up, standing at attention while the German commander walks down the line. Some poor starving prisoner has stolen a chicken and the commander intends to flush out the culprit.

"Who stole the chicken?" The officer barks.

No one speaks. No one moves. Terror is evident in the faces of the prisoners.

"Who stole the chicken?" The officer repeats with more force.

Still no one responds.

The commander takes out his Luger and chambers a round, once more asking, "Who stole the chicken?"

When no one responds, he puts the gun to a prisoner's head and pulls the trigger, killing him instantly. The man drops to the ground like the proverbial sack of potatoes.

The shock and terror of this brutal act are palpable and the tension hangs in the air for a beat or two, then a little boy runs up to the dead man on the ground and points at the corpse saying, "He did it!"

It's an amazing, twisted, and morbid moment that instantly and artfully provides much needed relief from the unbearable tension.

It's no wonder that the film won seven Academy Awards.

For the most part, and certainly for the important parts, everything should be *shown* dramatically, but there is a time, and there are proper techniques for telling which can enhance your story and keep it moving without losing the overall dramatic tension of the narrative.

There is never a dull moment in the unfolding, rapidly changing, active environment of a shamanic journey. It should be the same in the worlds that you create.

Moving From Place to Place in Time And Space

How do you move your characters around and put them through the normal paces of their lives in a believable way, while keeping the juicy stuff for fleshed out dramatic scenes? How do you give readers information that is not reader feeder, yet not fully developed scenes, while keeping the overall dramatic tension pulled tight for the major arc of the story?

While traversing the cosmos on a journey, shamans can move about through time, space and dimension instantaneously, sometimes perceiving multiple locations at the same time.

In fiction, a narrative transition is the link that connects the pearls of your dramatic moments along the string of the necklace that is your plot. Narrative passages can rocket your story forward while passing along *important* information. They can be as short as one sentence, or as long as several paragraphs, but if they go on too long they lapse into telling, causing the energy of your story to dissipate.

In the case of a passage of time, you can end one scene and start the next paragraph with the phrase "two weeks later", "later that night", or if you wanted to give more information you could slide into, "For the next six months..."

With a few words you have magically transported your characters through two weeks of dental appointments, bill paying, and talks with mother. This is the shortest form of the narrative transition.

For longer transitions, such as one prefaced with "For the next six months," you can take advantage of what the opening phrase implies. This is the time to pass on information that is important to the story, but does not warrant a full scene. It is also a good time to revisit the inner thoughts of your viewpoint character and paint broad strokes as to what he or she is all about.

For the next six months, all Mike thought about was the book he had submitted to his agent. Days passed in a blur of increasing demands from his day job as a postal worker, while nights he slaved over his keyboard, writing his next book, trying his damnedest not to ponder the fate of his life's work.

One more rejection would push him over the brink. He glanced at the shiny metal of the shotgun barrel and the voice came to him again, beckoning...

In this passage six months of time passed in two sentences. It's a short transition, but it does a lot of work. As soon as Mike glances at the shotgun we're back into a full on scene and the tension is immediately cranked up.

Vary the way you use narrative passages. You don't have to use direct references to time with every transition. You can use events, changes of scene and appearances to show a difference in time and place. "Eight beers later...," "Three bitter winters passed before...", Two coats of paint later...", Two flat tires and a blown transmission later, the van pulled into San Diego..."

Narrative transitions are effective for leading the reader smoothly in and out of flashbacks. With a few well-placed words, you can slide right into a flashback told as a full, fleshed out immediate experience and then transition back to "present time". A smell, a scene, a mood, a song, any of these things can be powerful transitional devices for transporting your characters through time and space.

The smell of movie theater popcorn brought Colleen back to the first time her mother let her go to the movies alone with Joe. Saturday night. Monster Night. She could almost feel his hand sliding up her thigh.

"Hey, what the hell do you think you're doing?"

"Colleen, I want you all to myself..."

Boom. We're into the story - full on dramatic scene.

To get back to the present you need to find another connection.

The smell of the popcorn brought us in. We're in the scene with all the attention on Joe's hand. How about another hand literally pulling her back to the "present"?

A hand touched her shoulder, jolting her back to the concession stand.

"You all right?" Tony said. A concerned look creased his brow.

"Yeah. Sorry. The popcorn reminded me of..."

"You want some?"

The flashback could have gone on for longer. Make the scene as long as it needs to be, then bring the reader back to the original moment by making the link and zapping them back.

You can also use transitional devices to connect characters and scenes across space and distance if you are telling a story from more than one point of view.

Jennifer looked up at the full moon and wondered if Jim would make it back from the cattle drive in time to save the ranch from foreclosure.

This would be the ending of one chapter from the heroine's point of view. The next chapter would begin with the hero's point of view.

The cattle drive would be over in a few days. Jim stretched out on his bedroll and gazed up at the moon, thinking about the ranch and the last time he saw Jenny.

Choose the time and place for these moments carefully. As the creator of your universe you have total control over time and space. You can change the order of events, the viewpoint, and the way they're perceived. Use your power wisely so that each word and phrase carries the greatest dramatic impact.

Brick Walls

You grew excited at the prospect of writing your masterpiece. You've done your research, your outline's done, and you're well into your story. After struggling your beginning has come together, and like magic your story's moving along effortlessly, borne along on the power of your enthusiasm.

You work at it, pushing one day at a time, but the further you get, the more your energy dissipates, until you wake up one morning realizing that the initial stage of the rocket has burned out and you begin to wonder, what the hell am I doing this for?

You're approaching the Sargasso Sea of novel writing. The mid-book dregs. Many a fair ship carried by favorable winds has foundered and gone down here.

You'll be somewhere in the middle and you have a vague sense of where you want to go, but you're not sure how you're going to get there. It feels as if you've been writing your story forever and every page seems to come harder than the last until the very thought of continuing to the end carries such a tremendous weight that your momentum stalls. Soon you're asking yourself, "What am I even bothering for? No one's going to read it. Face it. It sucks. I can't write for shit."

A brick wall has appeared between you and the completion of your project. You'd like to go around it, over it, under it, anything but face it head on, day after endless day, but there's only one way to get past it.

Through it.

This is an energetic conundrum, one a shaman can navigate his way through by understanding the nature of energy and how to master it. This is also the difference between a committed writer and a dilettante. Inspiration can only carry you so far, it's the perspiration that gets you to the end of the road. The formula oft heard quoted in writing circles is ten percent inspiration, ninety percent perspiration. That's about right. While amateurs wait for inspiration, professionals go at it every day by freeing themselves from the energetic trap of the mind and emotion by funneling the energy into their moving body.

If you persevere and make your way through the doldrums, then slowly, almost magically you will get a glimmer of the light from the end. The hope that it brings will spark your energy and start pulling you toward the climax, faster with each passing page, until you're rushing headlong down the side of a cliff, hurtling toward a conclusion that becomes clearer with each passing word.

Before you know it, the story is writing itself as if you are possessed by some otherworldly intelligence. Your eyes, hands, and fingers protest, but their resistance is futile when they go up against your all consuming, passionate obsession, until one day, before it dawns on you what has happened, you collapse and tumble back to the real world when you reach the end.

Congratulations. You have written a book. Whether or not it gets published is another story. The most important thing is that you've written a book; not something that too many people can lay claim to.

Endings

L ike a shamanic journey, all good things must come to an end. The ending that you have been directing your words toward should be inevitable, believable, and if possible unpredictable, yet when everything is said and done, it should make sense, and above all, it must satisfy.

All the plot lines must be tied together, and all the conflicts must be resolved unless you purposely choose to leave a few "loose ends" dangling for artistic reasons. Sometimes stories are open ended so sequels can be written and sometimes they are open ended because the writer wants to leave you hanging out over the cliff in mid-air, like Thelma and Louise. If a writer doesn't close the circle it's acceptable, as long as it was intended that way. In such a case the writer would have foreshadowed this ending so it falls in line with all that preceded it.

This is the denouement, the climactic final scene. You're making your major statement here, which is in many respects, the very reason for your story's existence. This final beat of your composition is the moment when it all comes together. This is what remains with readers, hopefully echoing through their hearts and minds with meaning long after they have finished your story. Where do you want to leave your audience? Hopeful? Humbled? Horrified?

Think about it.

There are other issues that need to be resolved as well. By the end of the story, your characters should have changed in some way or another. If you've done your job right, there will be questions that are raised or answered, depending on how you play it. Whether you raise or answer them doesn't matter, as long as you play fair with your readers.

Done properly, you have grabbed them by their emotions and gave them the best ride you could by creating and building expectations, then frustrating them, while delivering an alternative that is just as believable. Whether you leave your readers upset or contented is your choice. What is relevant is that you have left them high up on the believability scale. Is suspension of disbelief still intact?

You can be as wild and unpredictable as you want, as long as it all makes sense and you do everything in your power to keep the ending from being a cliché.

After you do get to the end, put the manuscript down and forget about it for awhile, then reread the ending and see how it leaves you feeling. Are you still laughing, crying, or just plain old rejuvenated? Do the words still move you?

Are *you* satisfied?

Rewriting

A wise writer once said, "There is no such thing as writing, there is only rewriting." Pulling your words from the subconscious for your first draft will deplete your psychic energy. Now that you have a diamond in the rough, it's time to do the work of cutting it. A large part of you will resist. So much energy has gone into your creation that that it feels like tinkering with it will do more harm than good. Taken to an extreme, some beginners believe that their words and stories come to them perfectly formed from their muse and the thought of a red pen defiling their holy message is a sacrilege.

When a shaman returns from a journey through non-rational realms and comes back to normal waking consciousness, he is overwhelmed with a jumble of thoughts, feelings, and emotions that need to be put in order so the rational mind can make sense of it. This is the period of post journey integration.

To get the maximum impact out of your words, you need as many different sets of eyes as you can conceive of to scrutinize them from as many different perspectives as you can imagine, which is similar to what a shaman does in his integration. He may even discuss his impressions with a peer. This is an important part of the process of developing and shaping good stories.

With each successive draft, your work will be refined, clearing away one pile of clutter so you can see the underlying clutter that was hidden by the first; peeling back layers of the proverbial onion. Maybe that paragraph on page three really works better as your opening. Maybe the scene with the two Dobermans and the belly dancer is unnecessary.

Each editing pass is like finishing a piece of custom woodwork. First the cuts, then the filing and working of the edges, then the coarse sandpaper, followed by increasing degrees of fineness until you're ready for the finishing coats of shellac or varnish. After the finish, there is still rubbing and smoothing, until you're down to the lemon oil and soft cloth that polishes your beautifully crafted work.

To bring different perspectives to the long haul of writing a book, you should work steadily at your first draft, writing every day, pushing hard past the beginning, through the mid-book slump, all the way to the end. Doing a long, sustained drive like this takes a lot of energy, and for most, this first draft drain cannot be sustained for more than five to seven pages a day. If you don't have the luxury of time and you have to work a day job, two to three pages is more realistic.

While you are doing your first draft of chapter twenty, you can be doing a third draft of chapter four and a second draft of chapter twelve. You will have the benefit of time passed which will give you more distance from your work and you will know what is to follow, allowing you to add foreshadowing and other details while punching up bigger scenes and moments with an eye toward a future that you now know.

In the first pass seek out unnecessary words. Ruthlessly pare adverbs and passive voice. "Was", "were", "just", "seemed", "almost", "suddenly" and other "ly" adverbs should be weeded out. Are you using adjectives when active verbs will do better? Are you repeating the same thought in different paragraphs? How many words can you cut and still say the same thing with more impact? Does every word carry its weight?

In your second pass, think about how the sentences and the overall narrative are flowing. How about punctuation and spelling? Does each sentence, paragraph, and word carry maximum impact? Does the length of each sentence fit the pace of the unfolding scene?

Computers and word processors are powerful tools for creating literary masterpieces, but seeing your words on the screen has its limitations. It can be like doing a math problem over and over again, repeating the same mistake. With each successive draft, print out your story or chapter, get out your red pen and go to work. You'll be surprised at how looking at it in this different format alters your perspective.

Working in this manner, you will fall into an evolving cycle that keeps you involved in the story, working back and forth along the spectrum, while at the same time moving forward. When you get to the end, you'll be ready to print the whole thing, doing a single, non-stop, uninterrupted edit from the beginning, clear through to the end.

Once you've done that, set it down and forget about it for a while. Read a good book, watch movies, and pamper yourself with your favorite indulgences as a reward for finishing the project.

When some time span has passed, you will feel ready for the final edit *before* you allow others to read and criticize what you've done. This edit is one that you will be even more reluctant to do, but it is a must. Not only will you be sick of the work by this time, but you have a strong feeling that there is not much more that you can do.

In this last pass, sit down with the printed out manuscript and your red pen and *read the whole thing out loud* to yourself. It will amaze you at how unfinished and bumpy parts of your work will sound. This is the best final test for punctuation, flow, and readability. If it sounds good out loud, it will sound smooth to the reader's ear.

After running through this yourself, your manuscript will be ready for reading by others. If possible, find writers who are your peers or better, then find readers who don't know anything about writing, but who read a lot. You can never get too much feedback. Encourage honesty and don't trust anything your loved ones say. Remember the praise you got from your first mangled attempts at art in kindergarten?

That hasn't changed.

Give them all copies of the manuscript and ask them to note anything that bugs them, no matter what, then forget about the manuscript until you hear something back.

Line Editing

When it is time to line edit, the law of the land is that less is always more. Newer writers tend to lay on the details hard and heavy in intense dramatic moments which slows down the action. In these peak critical moments, the more you leave out, the more you leave to your reader's imagination. This is the time to kill your darlings. Be merciless. Choose your details with care and let your reader supply the rest.

What follows is the start of a novel written by a beginning novelist. Notice how the dramatic tension and impact of the scene increases as more of the non-dramatic words are removed.

It was dark. He felt numb, and disoriented, then he opened his eyes and looked around.

About thirty feet in front of him several people crowded around a van. He walked up to them and craned his neck to see what was going on, but found his view obscured. When he tried to tap someone on the shoulder he jerked his hand back as if he were shocked. It felt as if his finger had gone through the person.

Steve examined his hand and gasped. He could see right through it.

He looked down at his body; it had the same translucent quality, but seemed otherwise unflawed.

He panicked. Without thinking, he walked through *the solid bodies of the people in the crowd drawn by an intense interest in what was happening with the van. When he made it to the front of the crowd he froze.*

A motorcycle like his lay crushed beneath the vehicle, with a mangled body twisted within the wreckage.

He *stumbled around to the other side of the wreck and found himself staring at his own blood-soaked, inanimate body. One glazed eye stared back at him; the other dangled halfway down his cheek.*

The sight made his knees give way. His body sagged as the darkness tried to claim him once again. He managed to hold on, but a wave of confusion enveloped him. He struggled to rationalize this experience as a dream, but it had a surrealistic quality that heightened its vividness.

A moment later the answer became clear.

I'm not dreaming! I'm dead!

The sight of his mutilated body was bad enough, but the final devastating blow came when he turned and confronted the ashen faces of Jeff, Al, and Jenny each drawn taut in grimaces of horror and disgust.

Steve ran to them screaming, but they didn't acknowledge his presence. Jenny buried her head in Al's shoulder and sobbed, while Al and Jeff looked on helplessly. Steve felt overcome with emotion himself and tried to speak again, but all that came out was a series of unintelligible sounds.

His despair quickly turned to anger, frustration, then a wave of hopelessness. He couldn't remember ever feeling such anguish.

Even in his emotional turmoil, he had no physical sensations. He cried without tears, feared without chills or dryness of throat. He felt nothing on his skin except a limited sense of touching as if his whole body were encased in a giant glove. Gone were the textures and temperatures of his normal life.

He could feel the pull of gravity holding him down, yet he had no sense of weight and his perceptions went no further than his emotions.

The initial shock wore off and the full weight of what had happened enveloped his mind like an unwelcome fog rolling in off the ocean. The impact of his revelation seemed unbearable, especially when he thought about the people he loved, particularly Heather. His longing for her filled him with an acute sense of loss, as though some vital part of his anatomy had been torn out.

The ambulance came and he stared mutely as the paramedics extricated his body from the wreck and put a sheet over it.

For clarity's sake all the changes will be lined out and additions are in bold type.

~~It was~~ **D**ark**ness**. *He felt numb and disoriented,* ~~then~~ **until** *he opened his eyes and looked around.*

~~About thirty feet~~ **In** *front of him several people crowded around a van.* ~~He walked up to them and~~ **Moving closer, he** *craned his neck to see what was*

113

going on, but found his view obscured. ~~When~~ He ~~tried~~ **reached out** *to tap* ~~someone on~~ *the* **man's** *shoulder* **in front of him, then** ~~he~~ *jerked his hand back* ~~as if he were shocked~~ *when it felt* ~~as if~~ *like his finger passed through the person.*

Puzzled, *Steve examined his hand and gasped. He could see* ~~right~~ *through it***, then he noticed his arm,** ~~He looked down at~~ *his body;* ~~it~~ *they had the same translucent quality*~~, but seemed otherwise unflawed~~*.*

Confusion enveloped him.

~~He panicked.~~*Without thinking, he walked* through *the solid bodies of the people* **in front of him** ~~the crowd~~ *drawn by an intense interest in what was happening with the van. When he made it to the front of the crowd* ~~he froze~~ **his world stopped.**

A motorcycle ~~like his~~ *lay crushed beneath the vehicle,* ~~with~~ *a mangled body twisted within the wreckage.*

He stumbled ~~around~~ *to the other side of the wreck and* ~~found himself~~ *star*~~ed~~**ing** *at his own blood-soaked, inanimate body. One glazed eye* ~~stared~~ *gazed back at him; the other dangled* ~~halfway~~ *down* **the side of his face, hung by a pulpy red mass** ~~his cheek~~*.*

~~The sight made~~ **H***is knees g*~~i~~*ave way*~~.~~**,** ~~H~~*his body sagged,* **and** *the darkness tried to claim him* ~~once~~ *again*~~.~~**, but** ~~H~~**h***e managed to hold on,* ~~but a wave of~~ ~~confusion enveloped him. He~~ *struggle*~~d~~**ing** *to rationalize this experience as a dream,* **only this moment had** *a surrealistic quality that heightened its vividness.*

~~A moment later the answer became clear.~~

I'm not dreaming! I'm dead!

The sight of his **own** *mutilated body* ~~was bad enough~~ **stunned him***, but the final devastat***ion**~~ing blow~~ *came when he turned and confronted the ashen faces of Jeff, Al, and Jenny each drawn taut in* **their own unique** *grimaces of horror* ~~and disgust~~*.*

Steve ran to them screaming, but they didn't acknowledge his presence. Jenny buried her head in Al's shoulder and sobbed, while Al and Jeff looked on helplessly. ~~Steve felt o~~**O***vercome with emotion***, Steve** ~~himself and~~ *tried to speak again, but* ~~all that came out was~~ **only** *a series of unintelligible sounds* **bubbled up from somewhere deep within him.**

His despair ~~quickly turned~~ **blossomed** *to anger, frustration, then a wave of hopelessness. He couldn't remember ever feeling such anguish.*

~~Even in h~~**H***is emotional turmoil* **tore to the core of his being, yet** *he had no physical sensations. He cried without tears, feared without chills* **and sobbed with no** ~~or~~ *dryness of throat. He felt nothing on his skin except a*

~~*limited*~~ **muted** *sense of touching*, *as if his whole body were encased in a giant glove. Gone were the textures and temperatures of his normal life.*

~~*He could feel t*~~**T***he pull of gravity*, **still held** ~~*holding*~~ *him down,* ~~*yet*~~ **but** *he had no sense of weight.* ~~*And h*~~**H***is perceptions went no further than his emotions.*

As *the initial shock* ~~*wore off and*~~**passed,** *the full weight of what had happened enveloped his* ~~*mind*~~ **being** *like an unwelcome fog rolling in off the ocean. The impact of his revelation seemed unbearable, especially when he thought about the people he loved, particularly Heather. His longing for her filled him with an acute sense of loss, as though some vital part of his anatomy had been torn out.*

The ambulance came **in a flurry of flashing red lights and frenzied activity.** ~~*And h*~~**H***e* **could only** *stare*~~*d mutely*~~ **in silence** *as the paramedics extricated his body from the wreck and put a sheet over it.*

In what follows, see how cutting adverbs, passive voice, and adjectives tighten the scene, while the active verbs bring more life to it.

Darkness.

He felt numb and disoriented until he opened his eyes and looked around.

In front of him several people crowded around a van. Moving closer, he craned his neck to see what was going on, but found his view obscured. He reached out to tap the man's shoulder in front of him, then jerked his hand back when it felt like his finger passed through the person.

Puzzled, Steve examined his hand and gasped. He could see through *it, then he noticed his arm, his body; they had the same translucent quality.*

Confusion enveloped him.

Without thinking, he walked through *the solid bodies of the people in front of him drawn by an intense interest in what was happening with the van. When he made it to the front of the crowd his world stopped.*

A motorcycle lay crushed beneath the vehicle, a mangled body twisted within the wreckage.

He stumbled to the other side of the wreck and stared at his own blood-soaked, inanimate body. One glazed eye gazed back at him; the other dangled down the side of his face, hung by a pulpy red mass.

His knees gave way, his body sagged, and the darkness tried to claim him again, but he managed to hold on, struggling to rationalize this experience as a dream, only this moment had a surrealistic quality that heightened its vividness.

I'm not dreaming! I'm dead!

The sight of his own mutilated body stunned him, but the final devastation came when he turned and confronted the ashen faces of Jeff, Al, and Jenny each drawn taut in their own unique grimaces of horror.

Steve ran to them screaming, but they didn't acknowledge his presence. Jenny buried her head in Al's shoulder and sobbed, while Al and Jeff looked on helplessly. Overcome with emotion, Steve tried to speak again, but only a series of unintelligible sounds bubbled up from somewhere deep within him.

His despair blossomed to anger, frustration, then a wave of hopelessness. He couldn't remember ever feeling such anguish.

His emotional turmoil tore to the core of his being, yet he had no physical sensations. He cried without tears, feared without chills and sobbed with no dryness of throat. He felt nothing on his skin except a muted sense of touch, as if his whole body were encased in a giant glove. Gone were the textures and temperatures of his normal life.

The pull of gravity, still held him down, but he had no sense of weight. His perceptions went no further than his emotions.

As the initial shock passed, the full weight of what had happened enveloped his being like an unwelcome fog rolling in off the ocean. The impact of his revelation seemed unbearable, especially when he thought about the people he loved, particularly Heather. His longing for her filled him with an acute sense of loss, as though some vital part of his anatomy had been torn out.

The ambulance came in a flurry of flashing red lights and frenzied activity. He could only stare in silence as the paramedics extricated his body from the wreck and put a sheet over it.

In this next editing pass, notice that there are fewer changes. As each layer is peeled back more underlying issues come to the surface while smaller problems may have been introduced that need to be refined and worked out.

Darkness.
He felt numb and disoriented until he opened his eyes and looked around.
*Several people crowded around a van ~~in front of him~~. He craned his neck to see what was going on, but **they blocked** ~~found~~ his view ~~obscured~~. ~~He reached out to~~ **Tapping** the man's shoulder in front of him, his hand jerked back ~~, then when it felt like~~ his finger passed through the **man's arm** ~~person~~.*

*Puzzled, Steve examined his hand**,** ~~and~~ gasp**ing** ~~ed~~. ~~He could see~~ **when he saw** through it. **Looking down, he saw that** his arm ~~, his~~ and body; ~~they~~ had the same translucent quality.*

Confusion enveloped him.

Without thinking, he **pushed** ~~walked~~ through the solid bodies of the people in front of him, drawn by an intense interest in what was happening with the van. When he made it to the front of the crowd his world stopped.

A motorcycle lay crushed beneath the **van's front wheels** ~~vehicle~~, a mangled body twisted within ~~the~~ **its** wreckage.

He stumbled to the other side of the wreck and stopped **again when he saw** his own blood-soaked, inanimate body. One glazed eye ~~gazed~~ **stared** back at him; the other dangled down the side of his face, hung by a pulpy red mass.

His knees gave ~~way~~, his body sagged, and the darkness tried to claim him again, but he ~~managed to hold~~ **held** on, struggling to rationalize this experience as a dream, only this moment had a surrealistic quality that heightened its vividness.

I'm not dreaming! I'm dead!

The sight of his own mutilated body stunned him, but the final devastation came when he turned and confronted the ashen faces of Jeff, Al, and Jenny each drawn taut in their own unique grimaces of **shock** ~~horror~~.

Steve ran to them screaming, but ~~they didn't~~ **no one** acknowledge**d** ~~his presence~~. Jenny buried her head in Al's shoulder and sobbed, while Al and Jeff looked on helplessly. Overcome with emotion, Steve tried to speak again. ~~but only~~ ~~a~~**A** series of unintelligible sounds bubbled up from somewhere deep within him. ~~His~~ **D**espair blossomed to anger, frustration, then ~~a wave of~~ hopelessness. He couldn't remember ever feeling such anguish.

~~His emotional turmoil tore~~ **Though it ripped** to the core of his being, ~~yet~~ he had no physical sensations. Gone were the textures and temperatures of his normal life. He cried without tears, feared without chills and sobbed with no dryness of throat. He felt nothing on his skin except a muted sense of touch, as if his whole body were encased in a giant glove. The pull of gravity still held him down, but he had no sense of weight. His perceptions went no further than his emotions.

As the initial shock passed, the full weight of what happened enveloped ~~his~~ **him** ~~being~~ like an unwelcome fog rolling in off the ocean. The impact of his revelation seemed unbearable, especially when he thought about the people he loved, particularly Heather. His longing for her filled him with an acute sense of loss, as though some vital part of his anatomy had been torn out.

The ambulance came in a flurry of flashing red lights and frenzied activity. He could only stare in silence as the paramedics extricated his body from the wreck and put a sheet over it.

Finally, the finished product.

Darkness.

He felt numb and disoriented until he opened his eyes and looked around.

Several people crowded around a van. He craned his neck to see what was going on, but they blocked his view. Tapping the man's shoulder in front of him, his hand jerked back when his finger passed through the man's arm.

Puzzled, Steve examined his hand, gasping when he saw through *it. Looking down, he saw that his arm and body had the same translucent quality.*

Confusion enveloped him.

Without thinking, he pushed through *the solid bodies of the people in front of him, drawn by an intense interest in what was happening with the van. When he made it to the front of the crowd his world stopped.*

A motorcycle lay crushed beneath the van's front wheels, a mangled body twisted within its wreckage.

He stumbled to the other side of the wreck and stopped again when he saw his own blood-soaked, inanimate body. One glazed eye stared back at him; the other dangled down the side of his face, hung by a pulpy red mass.

His knees gave, his body sagged, and the darkness tried to claim him again, but he held on, struggling to rationalize this experience as a dream, only this moment had a surrealistic quality that heightened its vividness.

I'm not dreaming! I'm dead!

The sight of his own mutilated body stunned him, but the final devastation came when he turned and confronted the ashen faces of Jeff, Al, and Jenny each drawn taut in their own unique grimaces of shock.

Steve ran to them screaming, but no one acknowledged. Jenny buried her head in Al's shoulder and sobbed, while Al and Jeff looked on helplessly. Overcome with emotion, Steve tried to speak again. A series of unintelligible sounds bubbled up from somewhere deep within him. Despair blossomed to anger, frustration, then hopelessness. He couldn't remember ever feeling such anguish.

Though it ripped to the core of his being, he had no physical sensations. Gone were the textures and temperatures of his normal life. He cried without tears, feared without chills and sobbed with no dryness of throat. He felt nothing on his skin except a muted sense of touch, as if his whole body were encased in a giant glove. The pull of gravity still held him down, but he had no sense of weight. His perceptions went no further than his emotions.

As the initial shock passed, the full weight of what happened enveloped him like an unwelcome fog rolling in off the ocean. The impact of his revelation seemed unbearable, especially when he thought about the people he loved, particularly

Heather. His longing for her filled him with an acute sense of loss, as though some vital part of his anatomy had been torn out.

The ambulance came in a flurry of flashing red lights and frenzied activity. He could only stare in silence as the paramedics extricated his body from the wreck and put a sheet over it.

In these editing passes, sentences are restructured and pared down to say things simply, attention being paid to flow, punctuation, rhythm and readability. At this stage it's ready for a rest, then when some time has passed it will be time to be read by a critic, or if you're lucky enough to have good people near, you're ready to read it out loud to a writer's workshop.

After getting feedback, more editing may be in order and after some length of time has passed, one more read through will give it another finishing polish.

Writing Workshops

There are many writers who shun the idea of writing workshops, and for them this may be the best thing, but by doing this they lose valuable input. Criticism, both good and bad, is a necessary evil in the world of writing. If you don't get it from fellow writers, you'll eventually get it from agents, editors, and if your work does find print, critics themselves.

For the most part the feedback you get from agents, editors, and critics will not be constructive, unless you have a professional working relationship with them, otherwise they don't care about making you a better writer. They're in it for the money and unless they see dollar signs, chances are they're not going to spend any time with you.

Writers on the other hand are some of the only people in the world engaged in a highly competitive endeavor with each other, yet most of the time they will go out of their way to help each other. There are writing workshops going on all the time, but to reap the benefits of one, certain criteria should be met, otherwise if you are a fragile beginner, more harm than good can come from it.

There are as many different styles of workshops as there are workshop leaders. Some simply lecture, others give writing assignments, others pick out select work. There is value in all these approaches, but none can come close to the beauty of a read and critique that has full participation and interaction between workshop members, the leader, and the writer doing the reading. This kind of workshop should have a solid leader who makes the final call on a piece of work, and the more experience they have, the better.

In this setting, when read and critique takes place, the word of the workshop leader has to be the law, otherwise, the group is in danger of turning into a non-productive bickering session where bigger egos with bigger mouths win out.

Big egos and big mouths don't make better writers.

Following this interactive approach, certain rules of etiquette should be enforced to reap the maximum benefit from the experience.

If you are the person reading your work, read clearly and at a pace that is a little slower than you think you should. Most of us read faster than we think, especially when we are reading under the scrutiny of others. When you are done, sit and listen to all the critiques, good, bad and out-to-lunch, *without responding*. The temptation to defend your work is strong, but it needs to be resisted. If you experience mortal terror at the prospect of reading your own work aloud, ask someone else to read it for you. Even if you are not afraid, this is a good idea. Hearing another's reading and interpretation of your work can bring great objectivity and insight.

Once the reading is finished, workshop members should make their critiques, then the workshop leader should sum the comments up, so the reader gets the essence of the criticisms. When everybody has had their say, *then* it is time for the reader to discuss their work with the others, clarify misunderstandings, and solicit suggestions on how to improve their work. If this structured format is not followed, the defensive reader can end up arguing and defending their work with everyone which is non-productive.

This approach simulates what happens when a book is on the bookshelf in a store and a potential buyer picks it up, reads a few lines and doesn't get it. In this real world scenario the writer doesn't have the option of standing next to the bookshelf to defend their work.

It has to stand on its own.

If one person has a problem with a passage, the writer shouldn't worry too much, but if two people have a problem, the writer should listen, and if three have a problem, the writer definitely needs to do something. If you've written a piece that splits the workshop down the middle and provokes a heated debate, you've obviously written something that struck a nerve. Good job!

As one who is critiquing, pick out the positive things in the work and let the writer know what you like about the piece, building on what they are doing right, then give constructive criticisms aimed at solving the problems you see. Though it can feel awkward, be honest.

Never criticize content. If you are pro-life and the reader is pro-choice, put your differences aside and listen to the writing itself. Is it working or not?

It's best to write down your comments and give them to the reader. They can be helpful later when they are feeling less exposed and have more time to consider things. Try to keep your vocal comments concise and to the point, keeping the idea in mind that your spoken comments are for the benefit of the whole workshop. If you have powerful, in-depth criticism that you feel the writer needs to hear, wait until the workshop is over, or there is a break, then pull them aside to elaborate. Don't go into great detail in front of the whole workshop unless you feel strongly that it is benefiting all. The idea is for everyone to learn from each critique, not just that one writer.

If you are serious about writing for publication, at some point your work will be subject to criticism. It is to the writer's benefit to get this as soon as possible from people who have their best interests at heart, instead of exposing your work to the slings and arrows of criticism aimed by those who are looking for reasons to find fault and reject it with no interest in making it better.

What to Expect From Critiques

There are two kinds of feedback to consider. Short term and long term. Short term criticisms are the kind you get in weekly writing workshops. These are good for fine tuning scenes, paragraph and sentence structure, characterization, and dialogue. Hearing chapters once a week, people miss workshops and miss chapters. The continuity, over all plot, structure, and transitions will not get good feedback and character development and growth are harder to track. Each chapter and scene can be awesome within themselves, yet they might not hold together as parts of a cohesive book length plot.

Although they can miss addressing long term concerns, weekly workshops help catch bad habits while allowing you to experiment with your day to day writing. Weekly meetings are also an impetus to keep you producing new pages to read at each meeting.

As you refine your work, do everything you can to make it the best that it can be, but remember, the more you work at it, the less objective you become.

Once you've done all you can, it's wise to take a break and let someone else look at your work while you forget about it. The more distance you put between yourself and your project, the fresher you'll be when it's time to take another run at it. The length of your work and who you have to draw upon for critiques will help you sort out how to deal with the feedback you get.

Seek out writers with more experience if possible, send copies to your peers, and if you're financially able, pay to have a *reputable* professional give it a once over. The stress is on the word reputable. There are a lot of sharks out there, including literary agencies who charge reading fees and give "boiler plate" critiques. Other so-called agencies have people on staff who speak with great authority without having a clue about what they are talking about. Many hire college literature and English majors who know everything about verb conjugation and sentence diagramming without knowing a thing about fiction writing. If you're not confident in your ability, this can be a damaging experience. Don't take any chances. Ask for references and get someone with a track record who has worked with a friend, or a friend of a friend.

Aside from the writer's perspective, seek out avid readers and persuade them to read what you have written and get their honest impressions. Writers are so intent on plot, structure, technique, and the seams that hold it all together, that they can miss getting the overall sense of the story the way a dedicated reader can. You'll get an entirely different perspective from an "innocent" point-of-view.

Listen to what each person has to say and keep all your notes together. Though the articulation will be different, you'll find similarities in what people say which will help you focus on problem areas. Description, motivation, character development, scene setting, relationships, storylines, and how the story events unfold will be praised or criticized. Take the positive and the negative equally.

This is the time to feed your subconscious. Plug it all in and keep your mind occupied while your subconscious wizard performs its magic beneath the surface of your daily thoughts. Let it bake for a few weeks.

At some point, you will get a sense of when it's time to lock yourself away and embark on your rewrite. You may have to rewrite some major scenes and create or combine others. This is where you do major nip and tucking while pulling the whole thing tighter together.

Still More Rewriting

You've had a number of people read your manuscript. Some of the things you suspected might need work, do. Other things you weren't sure you pulled off, you did. Parts of the manuscript gave your cross-section of readers problems voiced in different responses, some conflicting, some remarkably alike. You may have a few bleeding manuscripts, notes from your readers, and your own notes jotted down from verbal critiques.

There is a lot to think about. Aside from the "big picture" plotting and structure adjustments, there will be lots of fine tuning grammar, sentence structure, and plot points to be addressed. The task can sometimes feel overwhelming, but if you approach it methodically and trust your subconscious, it will all come together.

Once you have your notes focused, take the manuscript with the most in-depth criticisms and distill all the notes and comments from the other manuscripts down to this one.

Plan on at least three passes, streamlining and smoothing as you go. During these run-throughs you will have the advantage of going through the whole manuscript uninterrupted from start to finish, which will benefit the continuity of the whole. On the first pass go through page by page, addressing the notes on the individual pages, solving the smaller problems raised by the critiques, while making changes like adding or removing scenes which deal with the work as a whole. This pass should solve ninety-nine percent of your plotting and structural problems, along with deepening your character's actions and motivations.

Don't be surprised if your subconscious pops up with new scenes that solve a number of problems, particularly in the beginning of your book where the story begins and motivations are started. Lesser characters may take on greater importance and other characters may recede, or some characters may be combined while relationships will shift according to the strengths and weaknesses that the criticisms have uncovered. Chances are, more than half of your work will be within the first one hundred pages.

When the first pass is complete, take a breather and take another look at your notes. Have you addressed all the troublesome plot points, character relationships, and other weak places? If you feel like you have, give the manuscript another run through, this time concentrating on paragraph and sentence structure, pacing, transitions, rambling and unnecessary dialogue, and what details you can add or remove. Is every word carrying its weight? If any words, lines, or paragraphs, don't set a scene, develop character, or move the story along, get rid of them.

When you get to the end of this pass you'll probably be sick of your baby which means that you're close to being done. Give yourself a good rest, then print out the manuscript, find yourself a private place, and once more *read the whole thing out loud to yourself* from page one all the way to the end. This is the final polish where you'll see how it all flows. If you stumble reading it aloud, your readers will stumble mentally.

Invariably, you'll discover that your polished prose still has a few bumps. You'll see new ways to say things better, smoother, more to the point, and more eloquently. Some of the things you originally thought were elegant, will sound awkward and choppy. Don't be afraid to cut and rearrange to give the whole work a smoothness that flows easily when read aloud. These extra agonizing and redundant steps make the difference between a polished, professional quality manuscript and the thousands of flawed amateur attempts that try to pass as marketable fiction.

This can also be a major, contributing factor determining the difference between a sale and a rejection.

Synopsis

A synopsis is the literary equivalent of the infamous "Hollywood pitch." It's the same as a movie trailer or a commercial, except that it's written as a condensed message that conveys the meaning of something much larger than itself with a series of powerful images that will hopefully provoke someone enough to read further.

There are as many ways to write a synopsis as there are agents, editors, publishers, and readers. Some want one page, some want four, some insist on ten. If it's as high as ten, then it's not really a synopsis, it's more like an outline. A synopsis shouldn't be that formal. It should flow and deliver a punch.

You also want to be able to deliver your story in a one paragraph "elevator pitch" and as a concise one sentence summary similar to the one below.

Land Without Evil is a story about the conflict between the religious beliefs of the Guarani Indians and the Jesuits in eighteenth century South America told from the Indian's point of view.

You want to deliver your plot and story in a clear and concise way without giving away too many of the surprises, and you want to entice. Your words and your story have to stand out from the rest. Agents, editors, and readers will skim the synopsis the same way a potential employer scans a prospect's resume before they'll even take a look at the book. If they aren't hooked by it, they will not read the first chapter. If they do get hooked they'll read on. The writer has to be convincing and persuasive in his presentation or they will go down in flames.

On book jackets, other than the hopefully catchy artwork, it's the blurb on the back or inside cover. Think of the pitch, the blurb, and the movie trailer as one and the same. Spend some time reading nothing but the blurbs on the backs of books. How do they strike you? Any intrigue you? If so, how did they do it?

When you go to the movies, study what the big money studios did to pique your interest with their trailers. How is the material presented? Did they give away too much of the plot? Not enough? Keep both of these approaches in mind when you sit down to write your own pitch/movie trailer/cover blurb. It's one of the most important sales tools that you have, so you want to put your best effort into it.

Rhythms of Writing

The act of dramatic writing is an ongoing process that should be fluid and dynamic. The more it is practiced, the more it falls into a rhythm which is not so noticeable in shorter works, but follows a definite mental and emotional pattern, particularly when writing novels and screenplays. A fitting analogy is a vessel. In the initial stages of the project the writer fills their mind with information from research which stimulates plot ideas and fuels momentum to get the story going.

Once enough research is done, the urge to get the writing started will grow until the writer embarks upon their project, spilling forth plot and story ideas, emptying out the vessel as the story unfolds. As the work progresses there will be a sense of relief, accomplishment, and mild surprise as more and more comes forth. The outpouring will slow as the mid-book slump sets in, then at some point after the middle where the light at the end of the tunnel is conceivable, the pace will pick up and the emptying process will move faster and faster until the end of the project comes in a flurry of frenzied activity.

Suddenly the project is done, a burden is lifted, and a sense of relief settles in until the reality of the impending rewrite weighs in with increasing persistence until it cannot be denied any longer.

Once more, you immerse yourself in the world of your story, getting to know your characters, scenes, settings, and relationships on more intimate terms. At this point the emptying out process is done, but you will still be fully engaged with the story.

Eventually the day will come when everything that can be done has been done. All the critiques have been assimilated and the rewrites are finished. There is nothing left to do, but send your baby out into the world to see if it has legs or not. After spending so much time living with your story and characters, they have become a major part of your life. You have been with them day and night for months and they have been uppermost in your thoughts, even when you have not been writing. The intellectual and emotional investment you have made is powerful and now the object of your passion is embarking on a life of its own.

At this point, what usually sets in is the writer's equivalent of post-partum blues. Your vessel has been emptied, and *you* will feel empty. Your life will seem without purpose and a lot of what you do and experience will feel meaningless. The best thing to do is put your project out of your mind and do something else. As a writer the best way to do that is to start reading and researching your next book. The process of filling up your vessel will start the cycle over again, giving it momentum as it gathers, only this time, you'll have a better perspective, because you have already been through it and will know what to expect.

Every book you write makes you a better writer. The more you get to know and understand the pattern, the smoother it goes until you finally tame it and make it work for you. The major difference between published writers and those who never find print is the number of words under their belts.

Like the shaman's magical flight to other worlds, writing is an act of self-discovery. Each time you go through this cathartic cycle you gain wisdom that only comes from experience. Each time you fill your vessel and empty it, you cleanse your soul. Not only do you perform the act of writing, but you *become* what you do. A writer. Like your words, your very being changes when you live through the process of becoming.

Writing is an art of self-expression, and is in fact the process of refining yourself in that expression which is the same thing a shaman does with his life, which is an unfolding narrative.

Conferences and Conventions

It's been said so many times that it has become a cliché, but it is a truth that writing is a solitary endeavor. You spend hours composing and polishing your work until you come to the point where there's nothing more you can do with it. If you're lucky, you've had a writer's group to help you. After spending time with them, you may have risen to the top and you might even be the star, but you only know where you stand in relation to the other members of the group. You have no idea where you stand with other writers.

One of the things that happens in writer's groups is that everyone gets used to each other and comes to expect certain things, so you tend to lose fresh perspectives. This is the time to get feedback from people who want to help you, but don't have any bias toward you one way or another.

Writer's conferences are an eclectic mix of all levels of writers, from beginners to seasoned pros, including all points in between. Some come to learn to be better writers, while others come to "be" writers by hanging around other writers. Some work on the same handful of short stories or book chapters all year, reading them over and over again in their local workshops, then bring them to the conference to get their egos stroked and win awards. Some do not write a word all year, then come to the conference and lock themselves in their rooms, writing feverishly, missing out on all the lectures and workshops.

To gain the greatest benefit from a writer's conference, forget about winning awards and impressing people. It's great to have your work recognized and validated by others, but it's more important to listen to the criticism other writers give you. If you get raves, take it with the same equanimity you'd have if you got trashed. You will come in contact with different levels of writers and criticisms, some better than you, others only babes in the woods compared to your experience. All of them have something to teach you.

The professionals that are teaching there are part of a vast network that includes agents, editors, and publishers. Become part of that network. If one of the writers comes to your town for a signing, make it a point to show your support. If you attend a big conference, you'll hear from best selling writers who are living proof that success is possible. You will also meet agents and editors. You may even be approached by one. Keep your eyes open.

If you have a committed, serious attitude, you will gravitate toward people who share your passion. The best writers at conferences are usually drawn to each other because of mutual respect and admiration for each other's abilities. Seek out and treasure these people. They are your peers. Make them part of your network.

Writer's conferences are a world unto themselves. Writers meeting writers all working together to make each other better. Conventions take a different slant. If you write in any genres, you should attend the conventions centered around these genres. Mystery writers have Bouchercon. Horror, Fantasy and Science Fiction writers have the World Fantasy Convention and across the country on any given weekend there are numerous Science Fiction, Romance, Fantasy, Mystery, or Horror conventions.

Many of these are put on by professionals, but the smaller ones are put on by fans, the people who will buy and read what you like. Your audience. It's good to spend time among them. Learn what they like and dislike. You'll also have an opportunity to meet professional writers, as many are key speakers who are part of the attraction for fans. Some of these conventions are hotbeds of writing business. Book contracts are signed, agents meet with their authors, and editors come to seek out new talent. If you are trying to break into one of these fields it behooves you to find out what's happening in it. It's one more thing that gives you an edge over the competition. If professionals in the business meet you at these venues, they know you are serious about what you are doing.

As of this writing, I have been teaching at my two favorite writer's conferences for over twenty five years.

The Santa Barbara Writers Conference can be found online at:

http://www.sbwriters.com/conference/

The Southern California Writers' Conference can be found online at:

http://writersconference.com

A comprehensive list of writers conferences can be found online at:

http://writing.shawguides.com/

Building a Resume and Building a Career

Aside from the personal exposure you get from conferences and conventions, what is even more important is exposure in print. If you work hard on all your projects and do not submit anything, you will never sell anything. Nothing risked, nothing gained. There are writers who only write novels and there are short story writers who only write short stories. Some writers do both. This is the best approach.

Short stories are an art in themselves and in some respects are tougher than novels, as you have to get your characters on stage, make your statement and bring it all to a satisfactory conclusion, with minimal words and maximum impact. Writing short fiction is great for stretching your writing muscles. You can experiment with different points of view, styles, and techniques that will help you become more adept at writing tighter.

Aside from craft considerations, short stories are a great method of exposure and can act as "commercials" for your writing. Unfortunately, because of the explosion of self publishing and e-books, the short fiction market is withering on the vine, but small presses and literary magazines are still out there, publishing for the love of the written word. For the most part pay is almost nonexistent, but there are places to publish and put another credit on your writing resume. The more you have in print, the more credits you can add to your bio when you submit. When an editor sees that you have been publishing, they will be inclined to take you more seriously.

Even if a market is practically non-existent in terms of pay, your words will be read. Many editors and agents peruse small presses in search of new talent. Though the money isn't there, the prestige is.

Another benefit of this approach is the simple thrill of seeing your work in print. Acceptances for novels from traditional publishers has become increasingly rare because of the glut of self published work that has flooded the markets and thrown the publishing industry into chaos, but short fiction is easier to market. If your work is polished and professional, acceptances will come. These little victories can be lifelines of hope in the tumultuous world of publishing that can keep you afloat in an ocean of rejection.

What is most important, is that by writing and submitting, you will be building a body of published work which will give you increased credibility and respect, and you will be growing as a writer. Sometimes, higher paying professional anthologies will look to the small press for new work and will pick up the reprint rights, so a story that has been sold to a small press gets reprinted in a bigger, higher paying, more prestigious anthology. If you're lucky enough for this to happen, you may find your work alongside the big names in the field. People who read these books for the big writers who are in them will see your work and may discover you as a new writer.

As you move forward in your writing career, work on increasing your exposure with your growing publication list and your presence at conferences and conventions. This is especially true if you are working in particular genres. The professionals in the field will see that you are serious and dedicated about what you do.

The ease of publishing in today's internet based electronic print on demand and e-book world has fueled the ongoing collapse of traditional publishing and rewritten the rules of marketing and distribution. It's the same thing that happened to the music industry and the film industry is following suit. Now streaming video is eroding DVD sales.

Network as much as you can and market your self and your work. You never know when agents, editors, or movie producers might be in a conversation, the subject of which might be you and your work, especially if you're lucky enough to be known for your publications.

Traditional Publishing

In the wild west of today's publishing industry, literary agents are a necessary evil and are sometimes spoken of in a derogatory fashion in the same language normally reserved for lawyers and ex-spouses. These colorful observations apply to a select few publishers and editors as well.

Agents, like many publishers impacted by the self publishing glut are struggling to justify their roles, and unless they are entrenched in film and television negotiation, they are finding it harder to make deals for books. As in any field, there are great agents, solid and reliable, serious and competent men and women who are looking out for your interests and theirs. Unfortunately, because of the lure of fortune in publishing, there are also incompetents, pseudo-agents, wannabe's, posers, and sharks. Watch your back!

Anybody can be an agent. All you need is twenty dollars for a box of business cards. There are no licenses or authority, other than a couple of self-policing organizations such as the Association of Authors Representatives, Inc. at **http://aaronline.org/**.

These watchdog entities are put together by well-established, respected professionals, but membership is not mandatory. Finding an agent who is a member of one of these organizations does not guarantee that you will not fall into the hands of an incompetent. This is one place to start a search, though it is nowhere near as effective as a personal contact or referrals. You can also check the *Literary Market Place*, *Writer's Market*, or *Jeff Herman's Guide to Book Publishers, Editors, & Literary Agents*, which is one of the best resources out there, but the best way is through personal contact that you can bet by attending a writer's conference.

Getting an agent should be your first step to exposure for your novel if you choose to take the traditional publishing route. If you send your work directly to a publisher, chances are your baby will go to the dreaded slush pile, if it is read at all. Because of the imploding business environment impressed upon modern day publishing houses, the bottom line is more important than anything else. Money is the lifeblood of the industry. Editor's careers are at stake if they don't produce income, so they don't have time to read manuscripts that show no promise of commercial success.

Agents are the screen that traditional publishers use to filter out the overwhelming mass of hopelessly non-publishable hopes and dreams that constantly bombard them. Like editors, good agents have an eye for talent. Many of them are former editors. The industry relies on them for front line support in the manuscript deluge. The agents themselves have their own front line supports in the form of readers who are often college lit majors which can be a blessing or a curse. Sometimes these people have an eye for talent, but if they are relied on for critiques, the results can be disappointing.

Agents who do not make enough money selling manuscripts, or agents who are simply greedy will charge reading fees. This is where navigation gets tricky. If it is an agency with English lit majors doing the critiques, chances are you will get a flawed and inaccurate criticism which can be more damaging than good. There are English professors with PhDs. who can tell you all about sentence diagramming, nouns, gerunds, and literary structures. They are highly regarded experts in academia, but they don't know a thing about writing fiction. It takes years to develop the knowledge of craft that working writers have. If you are not confident and do not have strong belief in your talent, an in-depth criticism from someone who really doesn't know what they are talking about can be disastrous.

There are large agencies who advertise all their movie star/celebrity clients, listing the massive advances they've negotiated for the rich and famous. They charge a hefty reading fee to beginners and send back a "canned", in-depth, generic criticism written in such a way that a desperate beginner will interpret its contents to specifically apply to their story.

As a general rule, steer clear of agencies that sell critique services.

Having said that, I know of one well known, best-selling thriller writer who paid a four hundred dollar reading fee, rewrote her novel according to the critique and gave it back to the agent who promptly turned around and sold it for something like one or two million dollars, but that is the exception rather than the rule. There are also "agents" who have impressive credentials that turn out to be incompetent and unethical.

Before you submit to an agent, your work should be as highly polished as you can get it and extensively critiqued and rewritten based on input from your own peer and professional network. You have to believe in yourself and your work before you expose it to the slings, arrows, and predators of the world.

If you have not been out in the writing world enough to know professional writers who might recommend you to their agents, the next best way is to meet them personally. Most writer's conferences have visiting agents and editors who sit in on panels. Go to the panel and listen to what the agents have to say. Ask questions. If you like how they come across, approach them after they speak, but don't be aggressive. Give them a quick "pitch" of your novel.

They may say that it doesn't interest them, but chances are they'll tell you to send along the first three chapters and a synopsis. If you make a strong impression, they'll tell you to send the whole thing. Get their business card, then leave them in peace, unless they are doing most of the talking.

When you get home, start the query telling them how nice it was meeting them at the conference. Possibly put in a line that will help remind them of a shared moment you can call to mind that will help them put a face to the work. It does make a difference.

Many writers worry about big agencies versus small agencies, or New York agents as opposed to west coast or Midwest agents. With computers and e-mail, proximity doesn't matter. Producing money makers is what matters.

Smaller agencies who do not have the clout of the bigger ones, can give you lots of personal attention and are sometimes "hungrier" than the bigger ones, but they may have limited resources and connections.

The main thing is to find and agent who loves your work as much as you do. If they believe in it, they have a good chance of making a believer out of a skeptical editor. The union of agent and writer is like a marriage where the agent takes a major part in the birth of your baby into the world. If they are a good, loving parent, the baby will have a healthy and prosperous life. If they are negligent and incompetent, the delivery can be stillborn or aborted.

Submissions

When you finally narrow down your choices and have your baby ready, the time has come to send it out and you have to do everything you can to put things in your favor, because the deck is stacked against you. Agents and editors will look at your work searching for reasons to reject you. Don't give them any.

Follow standard manuscript format with margins, double spacing, name and all. Your submission package gives the first impression of you and your work. Think of it as a resume for a high-paying job. The cover letter should be concise and to the point. A few sentences about marketing or what you feel is its appeal are acceptable, but don't go rambling on about how great your work is.

It has to stand on its own.

If you are sending sample chapters and a synopsis, there are no commitments. There is nothing wrong with querying a number of agencies. Make each one feel as if they are the only ones receiving your work. Some people frown on this, but agencies and editors are notorious for losing manuscripts and dragging out response times. You don't know frustration until you have submitted and waited and waited and waited, until you finally call, only to find out that your manuscript has been lost. None of us are getting any younger.

If an agent asks to see the whole manuscript, then you should let them know that others are looking at it, *if they ask*. They may want an exclusive. The worst thing that could happen is that two agencies want your work. How many of us would like to have a problem like that?

In spite of its craziness, remember that publishing is a business. Don't allow yourself to be intimidated. Treat it like a business. Don't be afraid to make phone calls and inquiries, only don't make yourself a nuisance. A phone call with a follow-up submission is almost as good as an in-person meeting. Instead of a face, they can at least put a voice to the words.

It is not unreasonable to ask how long they will take to respond and it is not unreasonable to ask who they have represented and what publishers they have sold to.

Once your submissions have gone out, forget about them and move on to something else that will keep you busy. If you get any bites from your submission packages and any agents want to see the whole work, send it out and sit back for the first part of the *real* waiting game. If you've done your homework and you are marketing a good, solidly written, engaging story, you should get a nibble from somewhere. If an agent expresses interest in you and your work it is time to ask yourself some questions.

How strong does this agent feel about your work? Do you feel like they "connected" with it? Are they in love with it? What are their plans? Do they want you to sign a contract? How long does it hold you for? There are as many different business arrangements as there are agents. The going rate is fifteen percent of your advance and royalties. If you land yourself a good, competent agent, this is money well spent. Good agents will get you the best bang for the buck. It is in their best interests. The more they get for you, the more they get for themselves.

Publishing contracts are many - headed hydras. This is where an agent earns his or her keep. There are publishing rights, first North American rights, foreign rights, movie rights, electronic rights, paperback rights, audio rights, reprint rights, property rights, possibly even rights to characters, expressions, and logos. All are negotiable. All are valuable.

The best thing that can happen to a writer is that an agent or an editor sees their work as a hot property. If this perception arises, the agent will send it to more than one publishing house and put it up for auction. It is all in the perception which is subjective.

Agents and editors are looking for reasons to reject manuscripts. There have been some tight, well-written novels that have never seen print because the editors see the markets as flat and do not want to take a chance on something that falls into a *non-income* producing market. Much of what gets published is a matter of timing. Good ideas at the wrong time will miss the mark, while mediocre books at the right time will flourish. Poorly written books have become best sellers because they catch a certain fad or feeling of the consumer masses. Sometimes they become the fad themselves.

Your agent has to believe in you and your work. No one can predict what will become a best seller. Sure they can market the hell out of it and make it an event by stirring things up, but even this is no guarantee of success. If you are already a celebrity, your chances of this kind of marketing and sales are radically improved, but it is still no guarantee.

These realities are all part of the tumultuous world of traditional book publishing; a roller coaster ride with the highest of the highs and the lowest of the lows. One moment, it can be cold, meaningless, and depressing, and in the next, so full of hope and excitement that you cannot contain yourself.

Either way, up, down, light, or dark, it is never boring.

Self Publishing

S elf publishing has a disreputable past that harkens back to the days of publishers called vanity presses where writers who could not sell their work to established publishing houses could pay to have their book bound and printed. Though these books found print, in the commercial writing world, a vanity press published book was considered the "kiss of death" as the majority of what was published was not fit for publication by established publishing houses.

Book stores and distributors would not touch a vanity book. Legitimate publishers would not buy these books, so why would the reading public be any different? Aside from the obvious look and stigma of a vanity book that doomed it from the start, some people with financial resources self published by other means, but they faced the same problem of distribution and book store exposure, with the exception of the rare independent book store willing to take books on consignment.

If they wrote something specialized with a specific niche and toured and lectured on their subject, they could make money by tying their books in with their lectures, but success in the bigger world was unlikely and elusive. There have been rare exceptions like James Redfield, who self-published his first novel in 1993 to widespread popularity. *The Celestine Prophecy* follows a narrator as he embarks on a journey to find and understand a series of nine spiritual insights on an ancient manuscript in Peru. Redfield sold the first 100,000 copies out of the trunk of his Honda before Warner

Books agreed to publish it. As of May 2005, the book had sold over 20,000,000 copies worldwide and spent 165 weeks on the New York Times Best Seller list. Redfield worked hard for his success, but it was an exception and would not have happened if he had not sold so many copies out of his trunk before Warner Books saw it as profitable and gave him the marketing and distribution needed to make it a best seller.

With the advent of the World Wide Web and the explosion of electronic publishing in the forms of print on demand, known as POD, and instantly readable e-books, traditional publishing and its archaic models of distribution were shattered. Anyone could publish an e-book for nothing and print books for next to nothing. In many ways the slush pile that once filled publisher's storerooms has spilled out into print, muddying the waters of the book reading public and glutting the book market in ways that no one could have predicted.

Hordes of "not ready for prime time" novices saturated the market with poorly written works, thinking that they had written the great American novel, when in fact they were following the path of the vanity presses that published what was deemed unfit for publication by commercial publishers. The difference between then and now is that today everyone has access to global distribution through the Internet. With POD, a reader can order a book which can be printed and shipped in a matter of hours, or they can download an e-book instantly. Traditional warehousing and distribution channels, which were the only way to get into book stores have been bypassed, seriously impacting the exclusive realm of established publishing houses to the point that major booksellers like Borders have gone under and others like Barnes and Noble are struggling for market share.

It is interesting to note the rise and fall of these behemoths. Originally there were independent bookstores, then came chains of smaller bookstores in shopping malls like B. Dalton Booksellers and Waldenbooks. B. Dalton was eventually bought by Barnes and Noble and Waldenbooks became part of Borders. Soon after came megastores like Bookstar, which was also bought by Barnes and Noble, then their rival Borders took megastores to the next level. These stores thrived for a time at the expense of smaller book stores before being brought to their knees by the new emerging publishing paradigm.

Barnes and Noble has managed to hang on by establishing an online presence and jumping into the exploding e-book market with their own Nook e-reader to compete with Amazon's wildy popular Kindle e-reader and Independent bookstores are experiencing a resurgence.

In the industry, brick and mortar is the term that describes physical structures that are the retail outlets we know as book stores. There is no place for selling e-books there as e-books can be downloaded in an instant, practically anywhere on any device, including cell phones. This has inadvertently created another divide between electronic publishing and distribution, which has become a free for all, and traditional print publishing.

This separation has extended to electronically submitted POD books which are in a large part amateur works following the time worn path of vanity publishing, with some notable exceptions that have thrived in the electronic publishing world. This has made traditional warehouse based distribution, the long standing promised land of print books with its maze of warehousing, shipping, and return policies, the main route onto the shelves of brick and mortar bookstores.

Traditional distribution is harder to do with a POD book because of the reasons already mentioned, primary among them the ability to sell and make money, not to mention the massive resources that established publishers have to promote and market their higher profile books. If you do manage to get your books onto the shelves of brick and mortar stores, you still have to find ways to promote and market them against this massive competition.

On another note, many independent bookstores will take your books on consignment, especially if you are willing to do a signing event that brings more people into their store. Usually they take a 60/40 split of the cover price with you getting the bigger share.

There are many things to consider before deciding whether to self publish. Internet publishing guru and best selling author JA Konrath created a great list of pros and cons in "A Newbie's Guide to Publishing" on his blog at:

jakonrath.blogspot.com.

Traditional Publishing Pros

- *Wide distribution and more exposure*
- *Most offer an advance, sometimes a large one*
- *They do the editing, formatting, cover art*
- *Marketing power*

Traditional Publishing Cons

- *Take six to eighteen months before publication*
- *Price ebooks waaaaaay too high*
- *They have power over cover art and title*
- *Don't use the marketing power they wield effectively*
- *Pay royalties twice a year*
- *Don't involve you in many of the decisions regarding your book*
- *Difficult to implement changes*
- *Lousy royalty rates, between 6% and 25%*
- *Very hard to break into*

Self Publishing Pros

- *Paid once a month*
- *You control price and cover*
- *Publication is almost instant*
- *Easy to implement changes*
- *Every decision is yours*
- *Great royalty rates*
- *Anyone can do it*

Self Publishing Cons

- *No free professional editing, formatting, or cover art*
- *Fewer sales*
- *Less than 10% of current book market*
- *Greater potential to publish crappy books*

The Internet and social media are saturated with newly published writers desperate for any attention they can get amidst a sea of newly published writers desperate for any attention they can get. All of them try to capture your attention in any way that might make their work stand out from the rest.

Many of them don't sell anything, so in their hunger for recognition they reduce the price of their books to ninety nine cents or give them away for free creating the perception that the book is so poorly written that the writer cannot even give it away, and more often than not, that is the truth.

On the positive side you can get instant exposure (along with everybody else) with the possibility of book sales from all over the world. If you have written a good book and think you can find a way through the chaos of social media and the maze of Internet marketing to start producing income, then you owe it to yourself to give it a shot.

There are numerous companies that are more than willing to take you on a self publishing journey for a wide range of fees and services, but not all of them are reputable. What follows are the most popular.

CreateSpace

CreateSpace is a subsidiary of Amazon. With CreateSpace you earn royalties every time a book is printed to fulfill a new customer order on Amazon.com, Amazon's European websites, your CreateSpace eStore, or through sales channels offered with Expanded Distribution. A royalty is calculated based on the list price you set for the location where your book is printed.

Kindle

Amazon's Kindle e-book royalties vary depending on the list price set for the book. If you select the 35% royalty option, your royalty will be 35% of your list price for each unit sold. If you select the 70% royalty option, your royalty will be 70% of the list price, net delivery costs, for each eligible book sold to U.S. customers. If a lower price is matched, you will receive 70% of the sale price and 35% of the list

147

price for each unit sold to customers residing outside Amazon's 70% territories.

The 70% royalty option is only applicable for books sold to customers in certain countries. For sales to customers outside of the 70% territories, royalties are calculated at 35%. For sales to customers in Brazil, Japan, Mexico, and India, the 70% royalty option is only available for titles enrolled in KDP Select.

Smashwords

Smashwords will distribute your books via multiple online channels, including but not limited to the Smashwords.com web site, major online retailers, among them Apple iBooks, Barnes & Noble, Kobo, OverDrive, Scribd, Oyster, and Baker & Taylor which operates Blio, a popular e-reading app, and Axis360 which distributes e-books to public libraries, as well as txtr, mobile phone appvendors such as Aldiko on Android, Kobo on all mobile platforms, and other online venues.

Smashwords usually pays 85% or more of the net sales proceeds from the work. The earnings-share rate for sales originated by **affiliate marketers** is 70.5% net. For most retail distribution partners, Smashwords pays the author/publisher 60% of the suggested list price set for your book. These rates vary by retailer for sales outside the US.

Ship It and Get to Work on Your Next One

Y ou've poured out your heart, written and rewritten your novel, had it critiqued, rewritten it again and sent it out. If you have pursued the traditional route, whether it is picked up by an agent, considered by a publisher, or rejected and sent on to the next agency or publisher, you have no choice but to wait – and waiting can drive you crazy. If you are following the path of self publishing, then you will have more than enough non-writing details to keep you occupied.

You may still be in the throes of post-partum blues, which doesn't make things any easier. Take a breather, read a few good novels, watch a bunch of movies and allow your batteries to recharge. You may feel lost and aimless for awhile, but if you keep your mind and your eyes open and "feed your head", the momentum will begin again.

When it feels right, start poking around at your research. If you don't know what your next book is going to be about, keep reading novels and watching movies. Sooner or later an idea will form and the irrepressible urge to put words to paper will come upon you once more. If this doesn't seem to be happening, then take Ray Bradbury's advices and "sleep on it".

Take notes and let the "germ" of your next work flourish. Eventually, the plot and storyline will form and you'll be making an outline. Before you know it, your project will take on a life of its own and you will once again be swept up in the creative maelstrom that gives meaning and purpose to what you do.

Be a shaman yourself and seize the tiller of being in the world. Weave a reality that can be conveyed to others through a common medium that we as a society have accepted as our primary means of communication. Become the God of your world and take control of the lives and destinies of your characters. When we choose to create, we emulate whatever force holds the universe together and create our own universes which we control. This act of creation puts our thoughts into the hearts and minds of others.

Be a warrior, an artist, a storyteller, a salesman, a critic, a craftsman, and believe in yourself and what you have to say.

Keep your work out there circulating while keeping it out of your mind. All you can do is offer up your best effort, then move on. Starting your next project is important, because as an artist you will grow with each book, sometimes dramatically. If your children never find a life the first time out, nothing says that you can't rework them years later with more wisdom and experience under your belt.

Above all, remember this:

What is most important is the process.

Do the best that you possibly can, then ship it and get on with the next one.

Recommended Reading

Abrams, David, *The Spell Of The Sensuous: Perception And Language In a More-Than -Human World*, (New York: Random House, 1996)

Bernstein, Leonard, S., *Getting Published, The Writer in the Combat Zone*, (New York: William Morrow And Company, 1986)

Bickham, Jack, M., *Writing Novels That Sell*, (New York: Simon & Schuster, 1989)

Boswell, John, *The Awful Truth About Publishing*, (New York: Warner Books, 1986)

Burroway, Janet, *Writing Fiction*, (Boston: Little Brown and Company, 1987)

Campbell, Joseph, *The Hero With A Thousand Faces*, (Novato: New World Library)

Curtis, Richard, *How To Be Your Own Literary Agent*, (Boston: Houghton Miflin, 1984)

Edelstein, Scott, *Manuscript Submission*, (Cincinnati, OH : Writer's Digest Books, 1989)

Egri, Lajos, *The Art of Creative Writing,* (New York: Citadel Press, 1990)

Egri, Lajos, *The Art of Dramatic Writing*, (New York: Simon & Schuster, 1960)

Forster, E.M., *Aspects of the Novel,* (San Diego: Harcourt Brace & Company, 1985)

Frey, James N., *How To Write A Damn Good Novel,* (New York: St. Martin's Press, 1987)

Gardner, John, *On Moral Fiction,* (New York: Harper Collins, 1978)

Gardner, John, *The Art of Fiction,* (New York: Vintage Books, 1985)

Hall, Oakley, The Art & Craft of Novel Writing, (Cincinnati, OH: Writer's Digest Books, 1989)

Henderson, Bill, ed., *Rotten Reviews*, (New York: Penguin Books, 1987)

Herman, Jeff, *The Insider's Guide to Book Editors and Publishers,* (Rocklin, CA: Prima Publishing & Communications, 1990)

Jung, Carl, *The Portable Jung,* (New York: Penguin, 1976)

Jung, Carl, *The Undiscovered Self,* (New York: Signet Books, 2006)

Kesey, Ken, *One Flew Over the Cuckoo's Nest*, (New York: Signet Books, 1963)

King, Stephen, *The Shining,* (New York: Anchor Books, 2012)

King Stephen, *Duma Key,* (New York: Scribner, 2008)

Macauley, Robie, Lanning, George, *Technique In Fiction*, (New York: St. Martin's Press, 1987)

MacCampbell, Donald, *The Writing Business,* (New York: Crown Publishers, 1980)

Madden, David, *Revising Fiction*, (New York: New American Library, 1988)

McConnell, Malcolm, *The Essence Of Fiction*, (New York: W.W. Norton & Company, 1986)

McInerney, Jay, *Bright Lights, Big City*, (New York: Vintage, 1984)

McKee, Robert, *Story*, (New York: Regan Books, 1997)

McKenna, Terence, *Food of the Gods* (New York: Bantam Books, 1992)

Noble, William, *Make That Scene*, (Middlebury, VT: Paul S. Eriksson, 1987)

Noble, William, *"Shut Up!" He explained*, (Middlebury, VT: Paul S. Eriksson, 1987)

Pallamary, Matthew J., *Land Without Evil,* (Los Angeles, CA: Charles Publishing, 1999

Pinckert, Robert C., *Pinckert's Practical Grammar*, (Cincinnati, OH: Writer's Digest Books, 1986)

Provost, Gary, *Make Every Word Count*, (Cincinnati, OH: Writer's Digest Books, 1986)

Schwaller de Lubicz, R. A., *The Temple in Man*, (Rochester: Inner Traditions, 1981)

Schwaller de Lubicz, R. A., *The Temple of Man*, (Rochester: Inner Traditions, 1998)

Schwartz, Laurens, R., *What You Aren't Supposed To Know About Writing And Publishing*, (New York: Shapolsky Publishers, 1988)

Truffaut, Francois and Helen G. Scott, *Hitchcock,* (New York: Simon & Schuster, 1985)

Vogler, Christopher, *The Writer's Journey: Mythic Structure For Writers, 3rd Edition*, (Studio City, CA: Michael Wiese Productions, 2007)

Warren, Robert P., *All the King's Men*, (New York: Grosset & Dunlap, 1946)

ABOUT THE AUTHOR

Matthew J. Pallamary's historical novel of first contact between shamans and Jesuits in 18th century South America, titled, *Land Without Evil*, was published in hard cover by Charles Publishing, and has received rave reviews along with a San Diego Book Award for mainstream fiction. It was chosen as a Reading Group Choices selection. *Land Without Evil* was also adapted into a full-length stage and sky show, co-written by Agent Red with Matt Pallamary, directed by Agent Red, and performed by Sky Candy, an Austin Texas aerial group. The making of the show was the subject of a PBS series, Arts in Context episode, which garnered an EMMY nomination. *Land Without Evil* is in development as a feature film.

His nonfiction book, *The Infinity Zone: A Transcendent Approach to Peak Performance* is a collaboration with professional tennis coach Paul Mayberry which offers a fascinating exploration of the phenomenon that occurs at the nexus of perfect form and motion, bringing balance, power, and coordination to physical and mental activities. *The Infinity Zone* took 1st place in the International Book Awards, Nonfiction, New Age category, and was a finalist in the San Diego Book Awards

His first book, a short story collection titled ***The Small Dark Room Of The Soul*** was noted in The Year's Best Horror and Fantasy.

It's follow up ***A Short Walk to the Other Side*** was an International Book Award Finalist and a USA Best Book Awards Finalist.

Dreamland, a novel about computer generated dreaming, written with Ken Reeth won an Independent e-Book Award in the Horror/Thriller category.

Matt's work has appeared in Oui, New Dimensions, The Iconoclast, Starbright, Infinity, Passport, The Short Story Digest, Redcat, The San Diego Writer's Monthly, Connotations, Phantasm, Essentially You, The Haven Journal, and many others. His fiction has been featured in The San Diego Union Tribune which he has also reviewed books for, and his work has been heard on KPBS-FM in San Diego, KUCI FM in Irvine, KX 93.5 in Laguna Beach, television Channel Three in Santa Barbara, and The Susan Cameron Block Show in Vancouver.

He has been a guest on the following nationally syndicated talk shows; Paul Rodriguez, In The Light with Michelle Whitedove, Susun Weed, Medicine Woman, Inner Journey with Greg Friedman, and Environmental Directions Radio series. Matt has also appeared on the following television shows; Bridging Heaven and Earth, Elyssa's Raw and Wild Food Show, Things That Matter, Literary Gumbo, Indie Authors TV, and ECONEWS. He has also been a frequent guest on numerous podcasts, among them, The Psychedelic Salon, and C-Realm.

He has taught fiction workshops at the Southern California Writers' Conference in San Diego, Palm Springs, and Los Angeles, and at the Santa Barbara Writers' Conference for twenty five years. He has also lectured at the Greater Los Angeles Writer's Conference, the Getting It Write conference in Oregon, the Saddleback Writers' Conference, the Rio Grande Writers' Seminar, the National Council of Teachers of English, The San Diego Writer's and Editor's Guild, The San Diego Book Publicists, The Pacific Institute for Professional Writing, and he has been a panelist at the World Fantasy Convention, Con-Dor, and Coppercon. He is presently Editor in Chief of Muse Harbor Publishing.

Matt also received the Man of the Year 2000 from San Diego Writer's Monthly Magazine. His memoir *Spirit Matters*, which details his journeys to Peru, working with shamanic plant medicines took first place in the San Diego Book Awards Spiritual Book Category, and was an Award-Winning Finalist in the autobiography/memoir category of the National Best Book Awards, sponsored by USA Book News. *Spirit Matters* is also available as an audio book.

Matt frequently visits the jungles, mountains, and deserts of North, Central, and South America pursuing his studies of shamanism and ancient cultures.

WWW.MATTPALLAMARY.COM

BOOKS BY MATTHEW J. PALLAMARY

THE SMALL DARK ROOM OF THE SOUL

LAND WITHOUT EVIL

SPIRIT MATTERS

DREAMLAND (WITH KEN REETH)

THE INFINITY ZONE (WITH PAUL MAYBERRY)

A SHORT WALK TO THE OTHER SIDE

CYBERCHRIST

EYE OF THE PREDATOR

NIGHT WHISPERS

Made in the USA
San Bernardino, CA
12 April 2018